GIRISH SHETYE

illLOGICAL THINKING

IN C++ AND C++17 ADVANCED

BlueRose ONE.com
Stories Matter
NewDelhi • London

BLUEROSE PUBLISHERS
India | U.K.

BlueRose ONE.com
Stories Matter
NewDelhi • London

For permissions requests or inquiries regarding this publication, please contact:

BLUEROSE PUBLISHERS
www.BlueRoseONE.com
info@bluerosepublishers.com
+91 8882 898 898
+4407342408967

ISBN: 978-93-7018-423-7

Cover design: Daksh
Typesetting: Tanya Raj Upadhyay

First Edition: June 2025

Preface

I am writing this to explore knowledge in C and C++. This book is rich in example and most practical oriented approach with example for college students and few graduates that are employed in software development project. These projects can be embedded one or application based. I hope this book will surely help them to understand concept in C and C++ in most simplified way. I kept language of this book very simple and easy to understand. I first part it covers basics of C language and in part to it covers C++ through my understanding.

I dedicate this book to my parents both father as well as my mother. They are equally playing important role in my life. I also thank my friends who support me morally through hard time.

I also thanks my school and college teachers when I look back, I cannot skip them.

With this new release few references are from online sources. I deeply thankful for making content available.

I also thanks finally reviewer of this book Mr. Mohit, Mr. Jagdish, Mr. Atul Sir of Sinhgad College of Engineering which gives valuable inputs to improve this book.

Table of Contents

Introduction

C and C++ are two such a language and hold basis and construct that you must learn are applicable to any language like Java, Python or OOPs based, UI based. Since basic constructs and fundaments are same throughout languages. It will help learning computer programming no matter whats the platform we are using like Windows, Linux, OS X. Since these platforms are built using fundaments of such a language. Nowadays lots of improvement have been done in it to match or to facilitate software development work. Lots of efforts taken to simplify code writing. C and C++ have C98, C99 are basic and C++11 C++14 standards that where introduce later for native development using these languages. With addition of native support means same library written in C and C++ may be separately or together works on any platform like currently we have Windows, Linux and OS X, etc. The effect of using native tools where greatly reduce development work and only required is some platform specific changes. So, redevelopment work for specific platform have been greatly reduce in time and cost.

I recommend students to use Linux as a open source operating system to learn C and C++ programming rather using turbo compiler and Windows platform. You can download latest Linux operating system and install on your machine since it is freely available over internet. It supports latest C and C++ compiler. So, you are capable to exploit latest features of C and C++. This book is very specific about examples and explanations. Also, history of C and C++ is not covered since lots of information is available over internet any one can read over it.

Topic Covered in PART I

C Language Programming.

Chapter 1.
Introduction to C

1.1. Introduction

Before we start, we will see the structural orientation of C language. We must know that using any specific feature of language it requires 1. Header files available 2. Library to support to use available pre-defined and pre-complied and tested functions. 3. main () function as entry or starting point for program execution.

In general case we need not use library, most of the time it is directly available through compiler, programmer no need to link it to main executable. Example: library used for printf () function. But to use math library, we need to explicitly link with executable for successful execution of your program else it will crash at run-time.

1.2. Structure of C and C++

1. Header (s)

2. main () function and

3. Linking of supporting libraries to build final executable. If we miss any library linkage then during execution or sometime during compilation program error generates.

To compile C program on Linux we have following command:

gcc file_name.c -o final_exe_run;

then on terminal type ./final_exe_run under current directory.

```
#include<stdio.h> //header for printf function

void main() {                //main

printf("I am printing message on terminal"); //library function

return 0; // return type normally a function have, will see in C          //
functions

}
```

Save above program as basic_C.c and type

gcc basic_C.c -o basic_c

./basic_c under current directory or type

./a.out if -o is not used if compiled like,

gcc basic_C.c

What is mean by compile-time and run-time or execution-time?

Compile-time: Normally this refers to removal of syntax errors or errors and warnings that arises during writing of program thrown by C compiler. Until and unless we successfully remove it, compiler doesn't allows us to have binary or executable. Warnings can be skipped by programmer but a good developer also take care of warnings.

Run-time: Normally this refers to the linking of libraries required for successful execution of program. Example math library which needs to be separately link. Run-time sometimes called execution-time both conveys same meaning.Run time means linking shared libraries developed by developer that may be C or C++ too. If shared library calls are invoked at run time if proper calls are not found, application crashes at run time by say missing function call.

1.3. Comment in C and C++

There are two types of comments in C. First is single line comment and other is multi-line comment. Single line comment is used to explain code written in single line with two slash (//). It is very necessary to have comments in program to explain sections of code written by software developer. It brings clarification in mind about code written. Another is multi-line comment, used to explain multiple of lines written about code. In any case comments are nothing but explanations which are not part of program but used to explain it. So they must be ignored during compilation as well as execution time. Comments are ignored by the compiler of any language. Multi-line comment is as /* … */.

/* ….explanation …

.. explanation … */.

Single line comment: // ……

Multi-line comment: /* …… */

1.4. Case Sensitivity

C and C++ both are case sensitive languages. Means upper case and lower case letters are handled differently. Example like HELLO_WORLD() function and hello_world() functions are not same. They treated as two different functions by the compiler. C and C++ compiler is case sensitive.

1.5. Rule for programming in C

1. C is a case sensitive language. Upper case and lower case letters are distinct.
2. Execution of C program start from main() function.
3. Each function should have return type. If return type is not specified then explicitly void is mentioned in the header of the function name. It is a good practice to have return type.
4. Function name should start with alphabet but not with numbers and special characters. For long function name, underscore used with alphabets. There shouldn't be any space between any two alphabets mentioning function name.
5. Keywords or language specific words must not used as a function name. Keywords have specific meaning to the C compiler.
6. Header must be included before use of function call, usually it is specified at the top in file. For each function prototype must be defined before function definition.
7. Each statement ends with semicolon (;) in C and C++.
8. C language does not support OOPs concepts of C++ language. But C++ supports all the features of C language. Therefore C++ would be considered as a superset of C language with additional features like OOPs and Classes which are superior than structures in C. We will see when we discuss what they mean to C programming.

1.6 Summary

- In this chapter we learn three basic things that constitute a program is one header file (.h, .hpp), .c for C language and .cpp for C++ language.
- Above files are very useful when we work with lots of APIs and pre-compiled tool. Use of library or to include custom module in any software application project.

- Comments are useful in program to include non-executable code, description or behavior about block of code written by some other developer when working on projects.
- And lastly rules or protocols to follow when working on C and C++ language.
- 1.7 Hausaufgaben:
- Explain .h and .c and .cpp files in context of C and C++ programming language.
- What do you mean by intellectual property in case of library?
- What are comments and their types? How they are useful in large, multi-file projects.
- Write a simple "Hello World" printing program on console. Explain within structure and comments by applying its rule.
- What is mean by project code documentation?
- Google about mentioned topic for more skill development.

Chapter 2.
Lets begin C

Now in previous chapter we seen structure and basic rules required for C programming. In this chapter we are discussing more details about keywords and variables.

2.1. Keywords.

Keywords are helpful in constructing C language. They are basic building elements required to perform programming task in C. They have specific meaning to compiler. Programmer shouldn't use them to hold data or any user define purpose. They are reserved for C language.

Keywords are: char, int, long, float, double, case, for, do, while, switch, default, signed, unsigned, short, if, else, break, const, continue, extern, register, return, sizeof, static, void, volatile, union, typedef, auto, enum.

Each keyword has size to hold specific byte length of constant. E.g. char is used for 1byte of data. int is used for 2byte in old compilers but nowadays 4bytes are used to hold integer. All keywords are in lowercase in C and C++.

2.2. Variables.

Variables are used to hold data like integer, decimal or floating value, characters , etc. Variables are named memory locations in program used to hold data or constant. They get memory allocation on stack. Variable name should be meaningful. It must depict purpose of use. For example variable used to hold employee id should be declared as employeeId or empId.

Certain naming conventions to be follow:

1. Variable name must start with alphabet.
2. Underscore (_) is permitted at start and between alphabet.
3. Variable name must not contain any space and special characters like @,#,$,% etc.
4. Keywords shouldn't be used as variable name.

5. Lowercase and uppercase letters in variable names are distinct. e.g. “ABC” and “abc” are not equal.

2.3. Constant.

Constant in C is defined by keyword “const”. They are fixed in value once assign to variable. Any attempt to modify or change other than original place they define in program results into error. We can have integer, real, single character or string constant, E.g., const int empId = 001.

2.4. Tokens

Tokens are smallest individual units in C and C++ programming. There are six tokens in C. They are keywords, operators, identifiers, constants, strings, characters and special symbols.

2.5. Identifiers

Identifiers are used to define user defined types such a structure, array, functions, variables. Identifiers must start with alphabet, contains digit and underscore (_), must not have white space or space. Keywords are not permitted as identifiers.

2.6. Data Types in C and C++

Data types in any language represents storage requirement to variables. Since memory is limited, efficient use of data type results into better program development as specially in embedded systems. Nowadays for computer application sufficient memory is available. But in certain area and application specific programming, developer must select appropriate data types to meet memory requirement e.g. ASICP (Application Specific Integrated Circuit Programming) washing machine programs. The size of data-types are based on two specification, one is compiler used and another is size of address bus or processor used for development. If processor used is of 64bit and compiler used is 32bit then application developed is of 32bit on 64bit processor.On 32bit processor 64bit compiler doesn't function properly.

Basically three categories are specified for data types.

1. Built-In types or Fundamental or Primary data types.

2. Derived data types

3. User-defined data types.

Example:

1. Primary data types are int, float, double, char, void.

2. Derived data types are arrays, functions, pointers and structures.

3. User-defined data types are declared using typedef where built-in type used to declared variable along with variable name use to define variable, enums are used to define named constants. e.g. enum SWITCH { SWITCH_OFF, SWITCH_ON };

2.6.1 Data-types Storage Capacity.

Data-types Name	Storage Size	Range in Decimal
Char	1 byte	-128 to 127
unsigned char	1 byte	0 to 255
signed char	1 byte	-128 to 127
Int	2 or 4 byte	-32,768 to 32,767 or -2,147,483,648 to 2,147,483,647
unsigned int	2 or 4 byte	0 to 65,535 or 4,294,967,295
Short	2 byte	-32,768 to 32,767
unsigned short	2 byte	0 to 65,535
Long	8 byte	-9223372036854775808 to -9223372036854775807
unsigned long	8 byte	0 to 18446744073709551615
Float	4 byte	1.2E-38 to 3.4E+38 with 6 decimal places precision.
Double	8 byte	2.3E-308 to 1.7E+308 with 15 decimal places precision.
long double	10 byte	3.4E-4932 to 1.1E+4932 with 19 decimal places precision.

To know datatype size "sizeof operator is used. The expression is written as "sizeof(datatype)". So on some platform int shown as 2bytes or 4bytes. "limits.h" and "float.h" are two headers used for integer and real valued data types respectively to know size.

2.6.2. Variable Declaration

Variable must be declared before its first use in program. Appropriate variable data type must be selected to define storage in memory and type of info.

Syntax:

datatype variable_name = initial_value;

// This syntax for variable declaration.

Example:

int id = 9999; declares integer type variable with 2 or 4 bytes of memory size.

float interest = 0.5f //f is used for float type otherwise
// integral promotion to double.

double division = 160.12435;

char vowel = ‘e’; //char must be specified in single inverted quote.

string employeeName = “Ramesh Arun Boppamurthy”;
//string is specified in double inverted quote.

2.7. Tri-Graph Characters

Trigraph character sequence are those letters which are not available on some keyboards. To use trigraph in program, it follow certain rule of sequencing. Each character consist of two question marks followed by ASCII character. Refer below table representing trigraph. There are total 9 trigraphs in C.

Trigraph Sequence	Conversion Of Trigraph Sequence
??<	{ left bracket
??>	} right bracket
??(	[left square bracket
??)	] right square bracket
??=	# hash sign
??/	\ backslash
??-	~ tilde
??'	^ raise to or power of sign
??!	| vertical line

Trigraph will be printed on console or output window with the help of “printf” function call as mentioned here.

printf (“\n ??= Hello C ??= \n“); and compile your code with “-trigraphs” option. See below, gcc -trigraphs file_name.c

command to enable trigraphs without this option warning generates and trigraphs ignored by gcc compiler

./a.out //execute programe

Output will be:

Hello C

2.8. Escape Sequences in C and C++

Escape sequences or backslash sequences are use to format output. Sometime console program or even UI needs string literals. These are quite long in length, so to format it such as to insert new line we have “\n” to be placed before new line start. “\n” is termed as a new line character in escape sequence. They are followed by backslash (\ ) followed by escape character (n). So together “ \n ”.

Escape sequence in C and C++ are mentioned in below table.

Escape Sequence	Escape Sequence Meaning
“\n”	New line escape sequence
“\a”	Audible bell
“\f”	Form feed
“\b”	Back space
“\r"	Carriage return
“\t”	Horizontal tab
“\v”	Vertical tab
“\’"	Single quote
“ \” ”	Double quote
“\?”	Question mark
“\\”	Backslash
“\0"	Null character

2.9. Printing and Reading data in C.

2.9.1. scanf() and gets()

To read data entered by the user from input device such as keyboard on computer, a specific functions are defined. There are different types of input devices like UART, Analog sensors, GPRS sensors, CAN terminals, reading string and so on.

To read specific word inputed from keyboard we have "scanf()" function. We read multiple decimal values and single word using scanf. To read multiple words we have "gets()" function. This function read entire string inputed from keyboard. Now when you move from one language to another language functionality remains same but only function name changes that perform the same task like reading from keyboard.

Syntax:

```
int scanf(const char *restrict format,...);
```

Example:

```
int age = 0;
scanf("%d",age);
```

In this example scanf function read integer type info in variable of name age signifies age of a person. Similarly programmer can read integer, decimal and single and multiple character set info. With scanf programmer can read multiple inputs from console by specifying format is called format specifiers.

Syntax:

The function is equivalent to and with infinite size and stream of stdin, except that the newline character (if any) is not stored in the string.

```
char * gets(char *str);
```

Example:

```
char fullName[20];
gets(fullName);
```

2.9.2. printf() and puts()

On same basis mentioned in the section 2.9.1. printf() and puts() works. printf() and puts() function is used to print data on console of computer or display device. printf() prints multiple decimal values and single word whereas puts() print multiple words on console or display device.

Syntax:

```
int printf(const char *restrict format,...);
```

The printf is used to show info on console read through scanf usually. To show proper value related data-type format specifier is used along with it. Programmer can show multiple values with printf.

Example:

printf("Age Of Person Is %d", age);

In scanf we read age of a person, so how we print it on console is with the help of printf. similarly puts is used to show character sequence on console.

Syntax:

```
int puts( const char *str);
```

The function puts() writes the string s, and a terminating newline character, to the stream stdout.

Example:

gets(fullName); in above,

puts(fullName); //display full name of a person

2.10 Format Specifiers In C and C++

In above we have seen how printf() and scanf() works. Along with scanf and printf it requires variables to specify the format of variable under read or write operations. In C and C++ information is classify into different types such as character, integer, decimal or floating point operations and string type which is a set of character type with null ('\0') termination.

So starting from lowest size datatype,

%c This is used to read single character from console inputted by application user.

%d This is used to read single integer value from console inputted by application user.

%f This is used to read single decimal value from console inputted by application user.

%s This is used to read complete character sequence value from console inputted by application user.

%x This is used to read hexadecimal value from console inputted by application user.

%o This is used to read octal value from console inputted by application user.

There are many other format specifiers are available depending on type and memory allocation to variables like sign and unsigned(%u), and (long long (%ll)) type. These format specifiers are used with scanf and printf like functions.

2.11 Storage Classes In C and C++

In C and C++ each variables are define with scope of use and there life span in the form of visibility and accessibility. Depend on accessibility and scope of variable storage classes are provided by programmer to each variable. there are five storage classes are applicable to each variable depending on there usage to particular application.

1. auto

    This storage class is gets applied automatically to each local variable in c and c++. The variable may be of user defined type too i.e. object of class. Once auto storage class variable goes outside block i.e. { auto int a =10) variable visibility and accessibility get removed automatically called auto storage class of local variables.

    Example:

    { auto int countBottle = 0; is same as

    int countBottle = 0;   }

2. register

    This storage class is gets applicable to less and faster memory access variables. They are internally stored in CPU register for faster access. CPU registers are less in numbers comparatively. Mostly embedded application uses such as automatic washing machines application. Program is less in size and few register for faster response by application. If enough registers are not involve then stored like any other variable in available memory. Sometime stored in cache memory for faster access demand by application.

    Example:

    register int bottle ;

3. static

This storage class is gets applied to count number of objects or to track total objects pass by vending machine. It useful in counting bottles in bottling plant as infrared sensor information of number of bottles filled per day needs to be counted for packaging and dispatch department. They are initializing to zero by default and applicable to entire file in they are present. Visibility is in entire file in case of declared globally. There accessibility is present in particular block but life is in entire program. It retain its value in multiple function calls. In case of C++ static function only access static variables inside static function. In non-static function we can use both type of variables.

Example:

```
void countBottlesInPlant() {
static int bottleCounter;          // default initialise to zero
bottleCounter++;                   // bottle is counted by one
}
countBottlesInPlant();
countBottlesInPlant();
countBottlesInPlant();
countBottlesInPlant();
countBottlesInPlant();             // call five times
bottleCounter    = 5               // final output
```

Now, call this function multiple times and print counter value, say called five times, as per behaviour value to be one but because of static we get total bottle count equal to five because of visibility. We can provide initial value need by application.

4. extern

This storage class is gets applicable to global variables. Usually during creation of library reference to outside variable or function is needed. Normally function specified in particular file is required in another file outside its visibility or scope. With extern programmer gives reference to such function or variable where it required in another file than its actual definition are present. extern keyword allows to call such a function without inclusion of file of actual definition.

```
countBootle.cpp // another file-name
extern int countBottlesOnTray;
                               // another file required counter.
```

```
int Bottle.cpp                // original definition file
int countBottlesOnTray = 10;
                              // referred value 10 from here to
                              //countBottle.cpp
```

1. mutable

This storage class gets applied to class objects. If variable is defined by mutable keyword is use to change constant-ness of const member variable modified by const member function. This feature is only applicable to C++.

2. volatile

if variable or member variable needs to be stored inside cache memory for faster access volatile keyword is used by embedded programmer for to have faster access by application.

2.12 Summary

- In this chapter, we have seen what are the different attributes and tokens used to write a program and there memory ranges.
- We have seen primitive and user-defined data types such as char, int, float, double and array, struct.
- These data-types occupies specific size in memory allocation. Smallest memory allocated is of one byte that is for char data type.
- Sometimes its required to display tri-graph character on console. For example we have LED board to display tri-graph character as a fancy character.
- We discuss about different storage classes for variable declaration. There are five classes, auto, register, static, extern, volatile are used to determine scope of variables.
- Mutable is a storage class used by C++ and not C to override constantness. Introduce in C++.
- We discuss about printing and reading a single character or a complete line using printf(), puts(), scanf(), gets() respectively.

2.13 Hausaufgaben

1. Explain different keywords, variables, tokens, identifiers and constantness. Mentioned there sizes in bytes occupied.
2. Explain tri-graph with example.
3. Write short-note on different storage classes.
4. How to read and write information on console?
5. Mentioned tri-graph and escape sequences along with explanation in tabular form.
6. Write short note on mutable access specifiers with example in context of C++ language.
7. Write a program to underline static and extern storage class.

NOTES

Chapter 3.
Basic Functional Units in C.

It introduces different types of operators use to perform different operations on digital data by means of mathematical expressions. These operations can be arithmetic or logical or both depends on required output. So these operations are carried out by different symbols called operators. example +,-,/,*,% etc.

3.1 Operators in C and C++

Operators are classified into various types as below given.

3.1.1 Arithmetic Operators

Arithmetic operators are used to perform arithmetic operations on analog and digital data in electronic form at present in high level language like C. All operators not only arithmetic are operates on data in electronic form. These operators are available in the symbolic form such as +,-,*,/ and %.

+ is called arithmetic addition operation.

- subtraction, * multiplication, / division and % modulus.

  Modulus (%) is used to calculate remainder of division.

3.1.2 Relational Operators

As the name suggest relational operators are used to find comparison. So comparison relationship is used to execute specific code. It allows programmer or developer to make choice or decision based on relationship between data. Actually programmer decides what relationship operations to be performed on data. Its completely depends on application under development. These operators are also available in the form of symbol and used to make decision. Also called as decision making statement used in conjunction with conditional statements such as if statement that we see later.

< less than

<= less than equal to

> greater than

>= greater than equal to

!= not equal to

3.1.3 Logical Operators

They are used to perform logical operations between two or more than two relational operators so we compare or select code on multiple decisions. Logical operators are in the form of symbol and used for comparison of multiple decision or conditions.

The symbols have following meaning in logical operators as below

&& Logical AND operation.

This means logical AND (&&) compares two conditional relations and if both comparisons results into true then only logical AND gives true. If first condition fails then gives false and skip checking other conditions. so code under consideration does not execute on false output.

Truth Table of Logical AND Operation

Logical AND (&&) Operation		
Input A	Input B	Output (O/P)
A = 0	B = 0	O/P = 0
A = 0	B = 1	O/P = 0
A = 1	B = 0	O/P = 0
A = 1	B = 1	O/P = 1

| | Logical OR operation.

This means logical OR (||) compares two conditional relations and if first comparison results into true then only logical OR gives true. If first condition fails then gives false and check other condition. If other comparison results into true (only two conditions) results into true gives logical OR true. So conclusion is to logical OR gives true only either of the specified comparison results into true otherwise false so code under consideration does not execute on false output.

Truth Table of Logical OR Operation

Logical OR (||) Operation		
Input A	Input B	Output (O/P)
A = 0	B = 0	O/P = 0
A = 0	B = 1	O/P = 1
A = 1	B = 0	O/P = 1
A = 1	B = 1	O/P = 1

! Logical NOT operation.

This means logical NOT (!) converts results into its complement form. If the result of decision becomes true then logical NOT (!) converts it into false and if the result of decision becomes false then logical NOT (!) converts it into true logical operation. Logical NOT operation works on final result of expression. Sometimes it may happen that expression consist of only one expression and programmer wants to complement it. In that case too logical NOT (!) expression available and does same things as discuss above.

Truth Table of Logical NOT Operation

Logical NOT (!)	
Input A	Output (O/P)
A = 0	O/P = 0
A = 1	O/P = 1

3.1.4 Assignment Operator

Assignment operator (=) is single equal to sign symbol used to assign right hand value to left hand variable. Variable is on left side to hold value. Assignment operator is used with arithmetic operators to assign result of arithmetic operations. Assignment operator use for shorthand assignment means longer expression is implemented in shorthand.

Consider the following: a = a + c; so this will be written as a += c; This form of expression is called shorthand assignments. This will results into faster execution of shorthand expression as lefthand operand is already read in few steps so further expansion of expression is not necessary. This technique is used with other arithmetic operators in similar way.

Syntax for shorthand operator:- variable operator= expression i.e. a += c in this 'a' is a variable, '+' is operator followed by equal to sign and expression.

3.1.5 Conditiona/Ternaryl Operator

Conditional operator is also called ternary operator. It consist two symbols (?) and (:). It is called ternary operator since it is use to give result based on three expressions.

Syntax:

var = (conditional expression) ? expr2 : expr3;

i.e. var1 = (b > a) ? b : a in this ‘ b > a ’ is conditional expression. if it evaluates true then expr2 i.e. ‘var1 = b’ gets assign otherwise evaluates to be false and ‘var1 = a’ gets assign.

3.1.6 Decrement and Increment Operator

Decrement (--) and increment (++) are used to decrease value of variable by one unit and increase the value of variable by one unit respectively. These operators called unary operators as they act on single variable. They are classified in two categories one is prefix and postfix depending on position of decrement and increment operator. i.e. is before operand (++a) is called prefix position and after operand (a++). Basic difference between prefix and postfix is that prefix will increase value first and then assigns where as postfix assigns first and then increase the variable value. Same applies to decrement operator (--).

- There are two types of Increment (++) Operator

Increment (++) Operator.	Expression	Output O/P
Pre-Increment Operator (++a)	int a = 0; ++a;	a = 1
Post-Increment Operator (a++)	int a = 0; a++;	a = 0

There are two types of Decrement (--) Operators.

Decrement (--) Operator.	Expression	Output O/P
Pre-Increment Operator (--a)	int a = 1; --a;	a = 0
Post-Decrement Operator (a--)	int a = 1; a--;	a = 1

3.1.7 Bitwise Operator

Bitwise operators are use to perform bit manipulation operations such as shifting, complementing etc. Bitwise operators are applicable to integers, but may not use in case of float and double type.

Bitwise operators are below:-

~ bitwise complement operator

The operation of bitwise complement operator is similar to logical NOT operation with difference is that it works on individual bit of expression. There truth tables are same. In bitwise complement operation logic one is turn down to make logic zero and logic zero is turn down to make logic one.

Example: if A = 0x8f then bitwise complement of ~A = 0x70.

Input: A = 0x8f

1	0	0	0	1	1	1	1

Output: A = ~A is 0x70

0	1	1	1	0	0	0	0

& bitwise AND operator

The operation of bitwise AND operator is similar to logical AND operation with difference is that it works on individual bit of expression. There truth tables are same.

Example: A = 0x8f and B = 0x5b then C = (A & B) = 0x0b

Input: A = 0x8f

1	0	0	0	1	1	1	1

Input: B = 0x5b

0	1	0	1	1	0	1	1

Output: C = (A & B) = 0x0b

0	0	0	0	1	0	1	1

| bitwise OR operator

The operation of bitwise OR operator is similar to logical OR operation with difference is that it works on individual bit of expression. There truth tables are same.

Example: A = 0x8f and B = 0x5b then C = (A | B) = 0xdf

Input: A = 0x8f

1	0	0	0	1	1	1	1

Input: B = 0x5b

0	1	0	1	1	0	1	1

Output: C = (A | B) = 0xdf

1	1	0	1	1	1	1	1

^ bitwise exclusive OR (XOR)

The exclusive OR (XOR) operation between two input is to perform only when one of the input is connected to logic 1. To understand this situation when we have two bulb switches are connected in parallel and operators wants to on either of the bulb. So programmer or home automation operator wants to turn on either of bulb, we go for exclusive OR (XOR) operation.

In XOR operation when there is odd number of once output is high and bulb switch supply electricity in house.

Truth Table of Logical exclusive OR (XOR) Operation

Exclusive OR (^) Operation		
Input A	Input B	Output (O/P)
A = 0	B = 0	O/P = 0
A = 0	B = 1	O/P = 1
A = 1	B = 0	O/P = 1
A = 1	B = 1	O/P = 0

Example: A = 0x8f and B = 0x5b then C = (A ^ B) = 0xdc

Input: A = 0x8f

1	0	0	0	1	1	1	1

Input: B = 0x5b

0	1	0	1	1	0	1	1

Output: C = (A ^ B) = 0xdc

1	1	0	1	1	1	0	0

<< bitwise left shift operator

In bitwise left shift operator LSB i.e. least significant bit is shifted to left by one bit position. Zeros are appended to the LSB vacant position.

Example:

Here 0xff is left shifted by 2 bits, so after bitwise left shift operation we get following o/p. MSB bit get discarded by 2 bits as in example.

Input: 0xff before left shift operation

1	1	1	1	1	1	1	1	<<	2

Output: 0xfc after 2 bit left shift operation

1	1	1	1	1	1	0	0

>> bitwise right shift operator

In bitwise right shift operator MSB i.e. most significant bit is shifted to right by one bit position. Zeros are appended to the MSB vacant position.

Example:

Here 0xff is right shifted by 2 bits, so after bitwise right shift operation we get following o/p. LSB bit get discarded by 2 bits as in example.

Input: 0xff before right shift operation

1	1	1	1	1	1	1	1	>>	2

Output: 0x2f after 2 bit right shift operation

0	0	1	1	1	1	1	1

3.2 Expression in C and C++

Expression in programming languages are made of variables, constants and operators that are use to perform computation. One such a programming language is C and C++. Many other languages do exist that may have few additional component in expression i.e. Objects in C++.

Now to evaluate expression certain rules to be followed. To evaluates arithmetic expression BoDMAS i.e. Bracket, Division, Multiplication, Arithmetic and Subtraction to be evaluated in sequence. Bracket has highest preference and will be considered first for solving expression.

3.2.1 Rules for solving conflict occurs due to operators

1. Bracket has highest precedence. In nested bracket, inner most bracket have highest precedence and needs to be evaluated first.
2. Associativity of operator is considered when two or more operators are of same priority or precedence level appear in a expression or sub-expression.
3. Precedence of operator is considered during evaluation of expression or sub-expression.

3.2.2 Operator Precedence and Associativity of operators in C are summaries in following table.

<table>
<tr><th>Operator</th><th>Description</th><th>Associativity</th><th>Rank</th></tr>
<tr><td>( )
[ ]</td><td>Function Call
Array Element Reference</td><td>Left to Right</td><td>1</td></tr>
<tr><td>+
—
++
— —
!
~
*
&
sizeof
(type)</td><td>Unary plus
Unary minus
Increment
Decrement
logical negation
Once complement
Pointer reference
Address
Size of Object
Type Cast</td><td>Right to Left</td><td>2</td></tr>
<tr><td>*
/
%</td><td>Multiplication
Division
Modulus</td><td>Left to Right</td><td>3</td></tr>
<tr><td>+
—</td><td>Addition
Subtraction</td><td>Left to Right</td><td>4</td></tr>
<tr><td><<
>></td><td>Left Shift
Right Shift</td><td>Left to Right</td><td>5</td></tr>
<tr><td><
<=
>
>=</td><td>Less than
Less than equal to
Greater than
Greater than equal to</td><td>Left to Right</td><td>6</td></tr>
<tr><td>==
!=</td><td>Equality
Inequality</td><td>Left to Right</td><td>7</td></tr>
<tr><td>&</td><td>Bitwise AND</td><td>Left to Right</td><td>8</td></tr>
<tr><td>^</td><td>Bitwise XOR</td><td>Left to Right</td><td>9</td></tr>
<tr><td>|</td><td>Bitwise OR</td><td>Left to Right</td><td>10</td></tr>
<tr><td>&&</td><td>Logical AND</td><td>Left to Right</td><td>11</td></tr>
<tr><td>||</td><td>Logical OR</td><td>Left to Right</td><td>12</td></tr>
<tr><td>?:</td><td>Conditional Operator</td><td>Right to Left</td><td>13</td></tr>
<tr><td>=
*= /= %=
+= -= &=
^= |=
<<= >>=</td><td>Assignment Operators</td><td>Right to Left</td><td>14</td></tr>
<tr><td>,</td><td>Comma operator</td><td>Left to Right</td><td>15</td></tr>
</table>

3.3 Type Conversion in C and C++

Type conversion is a technique implemented or supported by programming language in which datatype is promoted to higher level automatically or need to be promoted to specific datatype on requirement of expression manually by the programmer. This is called type conversion in C and C++.

3.3.1 Type conversion is classified as below

1. Implicit Type Conversion: In this datatype is promoted to higher level automatically in users perspective but its internally done by the compiler. This type of conversion of datatype is called Implicit type conversion.

   Example: In expression (int + float + double) values are present. So after evaluation ' int ' will be promoted to ' float ' and ' float ' will be promoted to ' double '. So at last expression is in ' double ' type. So conversion to higher level is happen automatically as programmer doesn't play any role in implicit conversion.

2. Explicit Type Conversion: In this datatype conversion technique, promotion given need to be converted to specific type manually by the programmer to match operand available on the left side of expression. This type of conversion of datatypes is called Explicit type conversion done by programmer.

   Example: In expression (int val1 = (int) (int + float + double)) values are present. After evaluation it converted to ' double ' type but we need integer type (int val1). Convert ' double ' type to ' int ' type programmer need to specify in bracket int i.e. (int). In this way ' double ' type converted to ' int ' type by loss of precision of ' double ' type. Sometime some compiler may generate warning or error because loss of precision is results into loss of data.

3.4 Summary

- In this we discuss different operators used to perform various kinds of operation on user data such as arithmetic and logical operation performed.
- We seen what is mean by operator and different types of operators used in C and C++.
- We seen associativity associated with operators.

- We seen type conversion between same types of operators and their integral promotion.

3.5 Hausaufgaben

1. Explain what is mean by operators in C and C++.
2. Explain different types of operators e,g. Arithmetic operators, logical operators, conditional operators, increment and decrement operator etc
3. What do you mean by integral promotion e.g. built-in and runtime promotions.
4. What is expression in C and C++ context?
5. Google it knows more about it as an example.

Chapter 4.

Decision Making and Loops in C and C++

In this chapter we introduce statements that perform actions on user information. It is very similar to human understanding of specific situation and ability to analyze them. In the same way, we can perform analysis of digital and analog information in different context coming from sensory input. So we have decision making and repeating same decision on bulk of information we required those construct on which our application run.

4.1 Decision Making

Decision making is a process of executing code based on certain condition(s) on this group of functions executes to give output expected. This technique is called decision making in C programming. To explain decision making consider a scenario of home automation system. In this customer wants to on lights at 6.30 pm. Also turn on fan when temperature of room goes above certain Fahrenheit say 80F. To implement various condition of home automation system as an example developer needs help of decision making statement.

Decision making statements are below.

1. If statement
2. switch statement
3. goto statement

4.1.1 If statement

if statement is used to validate only true part of decision making expression. If expression evaluated to be true block following if statement gets executed. Now in if statement there is no block for fail condition i.e. false output from expression. Such a decision making statement is called " if statement". Figure below represent if statement.

Syntax:

```
if ( conditions ) {
```

statements .. }

statements

Figure below represent if statement flow.

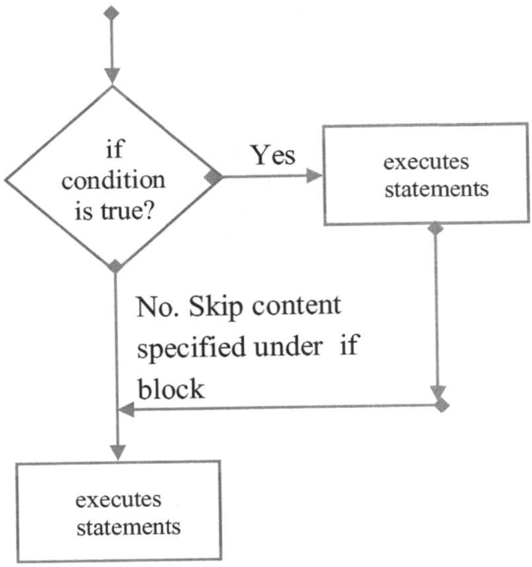

4.1.2 If else statement

If else statement is similar to if statement with added else part. In if statement we seen that it has only true conditional evaluation whereas in if else have both true and false evaluation. If statement part executes on true condition and else part executes on if condition returns false. To explain if else scenario consider home automation system in fan is either made ON or OFF. Easiest way to implement it is with "if else statement".

Figure below represent if else statement flow

Syntax:

```
if ( conditions ) {
        statements          // true if conditions validates
} else {
statements          // false if condition doesn't validates
}
statements
```

Figure below represent f low-chart for if-else statement.

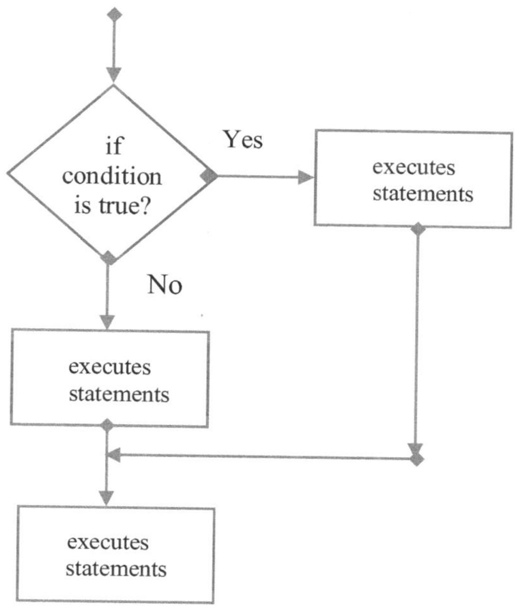

4.1.3 if else if statement

If else if statement have multiple decision making statements to validate more than two decisions. For evaluating two scenarios if else statement available. For more if else if statement used in ladder fashion. To explain if else if scenario consider home automation system in colour of LED lights to be changed depending on voltage levels. If 1V is applied across LED make it RED, if 2V is applied make it YELLOW, if 3V is applied make it BROWN and so on. In if else if statement, if condition returns false then only else if condition evaluates otherwise not. This is applicable to all if else if statements. Failure of one conditional block results into execution of successive blocks of statement.

Syntax:

```
if ( conditions ) {
        statements
} else if ( conditions ) {
        statements
} else if ( conditions ) {
        statements
```

```
} else {
        statements
}
```

Note: For above statement figure is similar to if else with more decision making blocks.

Example:

Following code snippet demonstrate if, if-else and if-else-if statement. To have only if statement consider if block, to have if-else consider only if-else block and to have if-else-if block consider whole example.

```
#include<stdio.h>
int main() {
    int isMAleOrFemale = 0;
    printf("Enter 1 to Say I am Male Candidate.\n");
    printf("Enter 0 to Say I am Female Candidate.\n");
    printf("Enter Choice = ");
    scanf("%d",&isMAleOrFemale);
    if(isMAleOrFemale == 1) {        // if block
    printf("Entered 1 to Saying I am Male Candidate.\n");
    } // if-else block
    else if(isMAleOrFemale == 0) {   //if-else-if
    printf("Entered 0 to Saying I am Female Candidate.\n");
    }        // if-else-if block
    else {
    printf("Invalid Option Selected. Run App Again.\n");
    }
    return 0;
}
```

4.1.4 Nested statements in decision making process

Nested statements in decision making process are required as developer needs to executes scenario based on previous output. In such cases nested statements are used. To explain this scenario in home automation system, customer needs to turn on lights first. if lights on then only turn on fan. if fan is on then increase speed of fan based on room temperature and finally give indication on LED by changing its colour. If any of the above condition fails like light is ON but fan is OFF then give appropriate indication to user notifying fan is not working properly and needs maintenance. So continue with other functionality of home automation system. Nested statements help in solving decision making process. In nested statements one condition is in another condition and so on is called "Nested Statements" in decision making process.

Syntax:

```
if ( condition 1 ) {                // condition 1 starts
        statements
        if ( condition 2 ) {            // condition 2 starts
                statements
                if ( condition 3 ) {        // condition 3 starts
                        statements
                } else {
                        statements    // condition 3 ends
                }
        } else {                // condition 2 ends
                statements
        }
} else {
        statements          // condition 1 ends
}
```

Note: For above statement figure is similar to if else with more decision making blocks.

Note: In case of large number of conditions, developer needs large numbers of decision making statements or needs nested construct. Now complexity of programming increases it becomes very much difficult to maintain code with comments.

To overcome complexity of coding means to understand code written by same developer or new developer (newly join in project) proper indentation and comments with proper explanation is needed very much in industry.

4.1.5 Switch Statement

Switch statement is similar to if else statement. It accepts integer and single character as an expression to select particular case. Programmer can't specify two or more character literals to switch expression. Switch case directly jumps to specific condition. if no case is selected then default case is executed. Switch case have only one default case. Each case statement terminates with 'break' keyword. If break keyword is not specified in each case then successive cases gets executed until break statement stop execution of cases of switch statement.

To explain this scenario with home automation system, in large projects implementation needs state machine meaning that application goes through various states like,

SWITCH_ON_FAN, SWITCH_OFF_FAN, SWITCH_ON_LIGHTS, SWITCH_OFF_LIGHTS, SWITCH_ON_TV, SWITCH_OFF_TV, SWITCH_ON_HEATER, SWITCH_OFF_HEATER etc.

To implement these various states of application we need switch case statement. It is inefficient to have if statement. In if statement we can not implement state machine required for application.

Syntax:

```
switch ( expression )       {
        case Case1:
                statements;
                break;
        case Case2:
                statements;
                break;
        case CaseN:
```

```
                statements;
                break;
        default:
                statements;
}
```

Example:

Refer section 4.3.2

4.2 Basic loops in C and C++

In programming world it is many times required to repeat construct working on same type of record or different record. One purpose of repeating construct is to retrieve records and perform operations on records. To explain this scenario with Swiss Banks has many financial transactions stored in server i.e. now a day's called cloud are used. This server contains lots of records. To retrieve records from such a remotely stored server we need to through individual record to get interested information and process it. Easiest way to implement is use of loops.

Loops are categories as below:

1. while Loop
2. do while Loop
3. for Loop
4. nested Loop

4.2.1 while loop

It is used to repeat construct based on specified condition. when specified condition executed to be true until these many times while loop iterates means repeats. Once all iterations are over based on specified condition then only while loop executed to false condition and stop further iteration and it breaks. In while loop specified condition is checked before iterations start. This type of loop construct is called 'entry controlled' loop. To explain this scenario consider a application in queue pattern for reservation of bus facility. In this information is taken out of queue based on queue is not empty. if queue is empty then do not take information from queue. It is a easiest way to explain while loop. One thing to be noted that in a while loop programer is unaware of size of queue so we need while loop rather than for loop. In this way it is better implementation.

Figure below represent while loop statement flow.

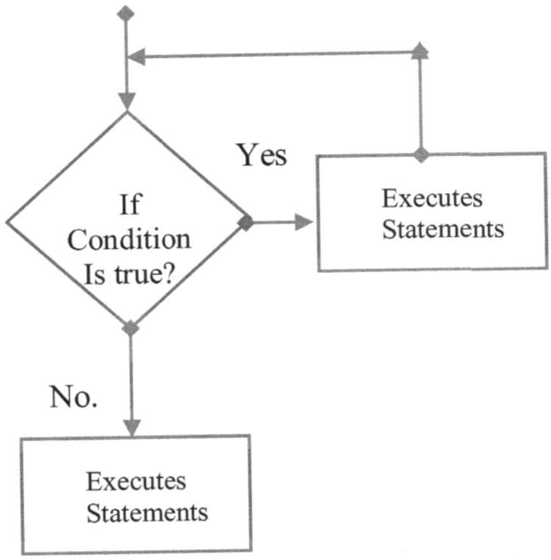

Syntax:

```
while ( condition is true) {
        statements;
}
statements;
```

4.2.2 do while loop

It is similar to while loop but with only difference that condition is executed after first execution of statements. Afterward executed if specified condition is true otherwise stop further iteration and it breaks. This type of loop is called ' exit controlled ' loop. To explain this scenario programmer need to execute nested construct i.e. while loop inside do while loop. Do while loop is best example of choice based console application. In console base application in initial days where GUI components are under development do while are jointly used with while loop. It is easiest way to explain do while loop. In this way its better implementation.

Figure below represent do-while loop statement flow.

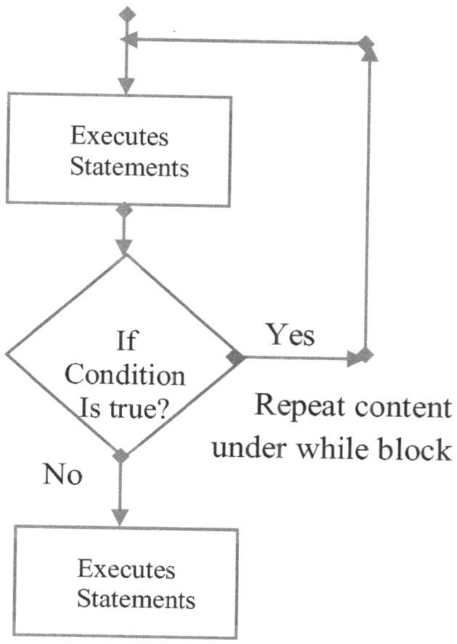

Syntax:

```
do {
        statements;
} while ( condition is true );
```

4.2.3 For loop

It is use for specific number of iterations. It contains three conditional parts, initialisation, condition for iteration and increment / decrement condition to have specific iterations. To explain this scenario consider a home automation in on single button press ON FAN, ON LED lights and OPEN WINDOW. Now consider FAN , LED lights and WINDOW are three objects always. This total size of objects is fixed. So in that case developer no need to iterate using while loop. It have better implementation using ' for ' loop results into faster processing of statements.

Syntax:

```
for ( initialisation; condition; inc/ dec condition ) {
        statements;
}
```

Example:

```
for (count i = 1;count<=3;count++) {
printf("%d",count);
}
```

Now in above syntax on execution of for loop statement it first initialise loop variable say count = 1; then it check condition say count <= 3; found true in comparison with initialisation, then executes statements specified in body of loop; lastly it increments or decrements condition say count++; then count value is incremented by one from specified initial condition say count = 2; then again condition is validated found true executes body until conditional statements gives false and loop ends.

4.2.4 Nested loops meaning loop inside loop.

Suppose for loop is inside for loop, in that case inner most loop executes first completely and then outer loop executes completely. To explain this scenario consider a home automation system in delay needs to be introduce. The delay effect is to synchronise between switching LED lights speed with switching FAN ON. It should happen at same instant. But switching ON LED lights is faster than switching FAN ON. To fix issue of synchronisation developer needs to introduce delay by nested loops. It is easiest way to implement nested loops. This way it have better implementation.

Syntax:

```
for ( initialisation; condition; inc/ dec condition ) {
        statements;
    for ( initialisation; condition; inc/ dec condition ) {
        statements;
        }
}
```

Example:

```
for (int count = 1;count<=10;count++) {
        for (int num = 1;num<=10;num++) {
        printf(" %d * %d = %d \n",count,num,(count * num));
```

```
}
printf("\n");
}
```

Following nested loop prints table upto ten. So bottom line is inner loop executes first and then outer loop. So total interactions will be multiplication or number of rows into columns. Usually nested loops are used to introduce delays in program. These delays of the order of few milliseconds or seconds.

4.3 Continue and Break statement

1. continue statement

2. break statement

4.3.1 continue statement

It is used in conjunctions with loop statement. Loop is used to iterate over records. Sometimes iterating in loop required to skip execution based on specific scenario. To explain this scenario consider a home automation system on customer needs to on LED lights, FAN but not TV. Now consider TV object is in list at 2nd index. so when we iterate over loop developer must use along with conditional statement a ‘ continue ‘ statement needed. It is easiest way to implement continue statement. This way it have better implementation.

Figure below represent continue statement flow.

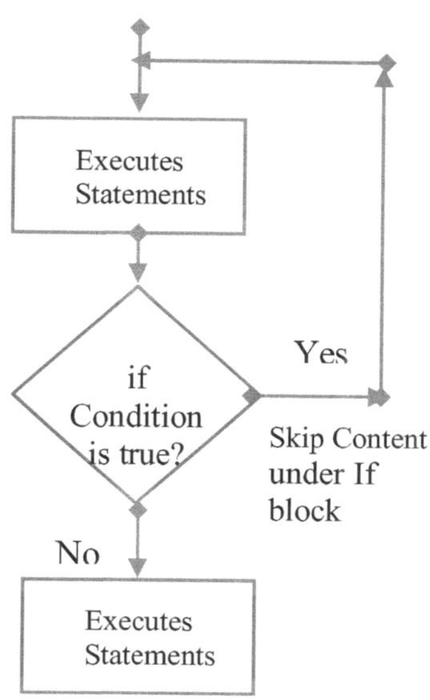

Syntax:

```
while ( condition is true ) {
        statements;
        if ( condition is true ) {
                continue;          // skip further iterations
        }
        statements;
}
```

4.3.2 break statement

It is used in conjunction with loop statement. Loop is used to iterate over records. Many times it is required to discontinue execution of loop at specific condition. To explain this scenario consider a home automation system based on customer needs to pay electricity bill. Now many electricity consumer records needs to check and specific consumer notified about electricity bill. Then in this scenario after notify loop needs to stop its iterations. The only way to stop iterations of loop is a use of ' break ' statement. It is easiest way to implement break statement. This way it have better implementation.

Syntax:

```
while ( condition is true ) {
        statements;
        if ( condition is true ) {
                break;          // it stops further iterations
        }
        statement;
```

Figure below represent break statement inside loop where loop is absent.

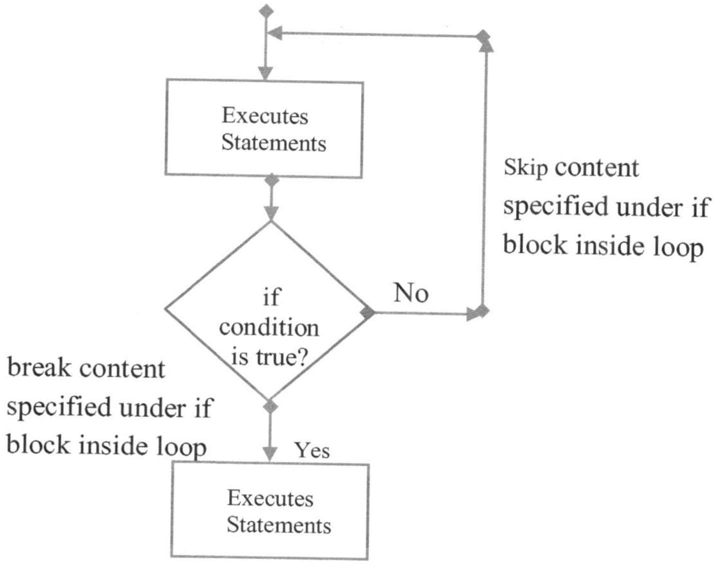

Example:

Following code snippet demonstrate switch case, enum, do-while loop, functions and if-else statement, break statement inside switch case and comparison operator and logical operator (&&)

```
#include<stdio.h>

enum LEDs {

        KITCHEN_LED=1,

        HALL_LED=2,

        BEDROOM_LED=3,

        BATHROOM_LED=4

};

void switchToRoom(const int choice) {

        switch (choice) {

        case KITCHEN_LED:

                printf("You are in kitchen.\n");

                printf("KITCHEN LEDs are On\n");

                break;
```

```
        case HALL_LED:
                printf("You are in Hall.\n");
                printf("HALL LEDs are On\n");
                break;
        case BEDROOM_LED:
                printf("You are in Bedroom.\n");
                printf("BEDROOM LEDs are On\n");
        .       break;
        case BATHROOM_LED:
                printf("You are in Bathroom.\n");
                printf("BATHROOM LEDs are On\n");
                break;
        default:
                printf("House is closed LEDs are Off\n");
        }
}
int main() {
        int choice = 0;
        printf("Get Inside House.\n");
        do {
                printf("1.Get Inside Kitchen\n");
                printf("2.Get Inside Hall\n");
                printf("3.Get Inside Bedroom\n");
                printf("4.Get Inside Bathroom\n");
                printf("0.House is closed. Exit App\n");
                scanf("%d",&choice);
                if (choice >=1 && choice <=4)
```

```
                switchToRoom(choice);
                else
                choice = 0; //exit house

        }while (choice !=0);
return 0;
}
```

Above example demonstrate ON/OFF of LEDS when particular room is entered by customer.

Note: Refer chapter 13 for example

4.4 Summary

- In this chapter we have seen decision making statements and loop statements.
- Many times it is required to take some decision based on previous, current or upcoming i.e. future events.
- Certain events required repetition or execution of certain events again and again, for example pattern changing disco LED lights. It changes color as well as pattern of execution with certain delay and repetition.
- So decision making and loop construct are very useful. They save time and repetitive work of writing code.
- We can specify multiple conditions to filter information.
- If, if-else and if-else-if, switch are used in decision making and while, do-while, goto, continue and for construct to repeat or skip, repetitive logic.

4.5 Hausaufgaben

1. Write a program to compare three numbers using if-else block and ternary operator (? :). Program to find minimum and maximum number and say "Hello, I am Older" if number one is bigger otherwise if number two is bigger say "Hello, I am entering 50th" else "Hello, I am 30th, Younger than all you".

2. Write a program to shift its bit (consider any number) and validate that number is present by bit validation.

3. Using switch case and while loop convert 100 to “one hundred”, 99 to “ninety nine”, 49 to “forty nine”, 13 to “thirteen” and so on up to 100.

4. Write a program to find prime numbers up to 1000 and there sum.

5. Write a program to find Fibonacci series up to 100 and their sum.

6. Write a program to find Fibonacci triangle up to 100.

7. Write a program to check biggest digit as well as smallest digit between mentioned numbers. Say 1234567 so biggest digit is 7 and smallest is 1. Say another number 786941 biggest is 9 and smallest is 2.

8. Write a program to check given number is palindrome or not. Also print palindrome numbers up to 1000.

9. Print Following pattern on console. Hint: Use 4 blocks of for loop independent to each other.

```
***********
***** *****
****   ****
***     ***
**       **
*         *
**       **
***     ***
****   ****
***** *****
***********
```

10. Write a program to see inputted number is Armstrong number and display the same up to 1000.

Chapter 5.
Arrays in C and C++

Introduction

Arrays in programming language uses to store many records of same type depending on the size of array. Array size is fixed means won't grow beyond specified size. In modern programming technique to hold large record array is not that much efficient. Array is used to hold few records. Database is a new technique now a days to maintain large data. These data stored on server either locally or remotely. To explain this scenario consider a home automation system in programmer knows at some places fixed size data collection is required. The property of array is that it stores same type of data i.e. int, char etc. Now the biggest problem with such technique to store record is different array of datatypes are required may be same or different size. If array size is same then it is easy to perform operations on data since easy to iterate. But if data are of heterogeneous type then use of array is a complete failure and it is very difficult for perform operation on data at same time like iterating over loop. Array is a collection of homogeneous information stored in same type of datatype with fixed size. Arrays are allocated temporary memory in stack. Once the scope of array is removed temporary memory allocated by compiler to array from stack is cleared. In this way we get back memory allocated on stack for further application requirement. Otherwise application will crash if no sufficient stack allocation made. Other approach to use of heap for memory allocation that we will discuss later. Array elements are stored in memory at continues memory locations. First element in array is stored at index zero [0] and last element is stored at index [size - 1]. One important thing lastly to say that datatype of array indicates what largest integer is stored at one position in an array. To hold large value we have ‘ long int ‘ and ‘ long double ‘ to hold real values.

5.1 Array Types

1. Single Dimensional
2. Two Dimensional
3. Multiple Dimensional

5.1.1 Single dimensional array

It have only one size element specified in square bracket. First element of array is at index 0. There is no negative (-) index in array i.e. -1.

Syntax:

datatype array_variable [size as integer];

Example:

int items [31];

5.1.2 Two dimensional array

It have two size elements specified in each square bracket. First element of array is at index [0][0].

Syntax:

datatype array_variable [size] [size];

Example:

int items [31] [31];

In above there are total (31 * 31) size elements are present.

5.1.3 Multi dimensional array

It have size specified with more than two elements specified in square bracket.

Syntax:

datatype array_variable [size] [size] [size];

Example:

int items [31] [31] [31];

5.2 Initialisation Of Array

5.2.1 Initialisation Of Single Dimensional Array.

In example 5.1.1 can be specified below

int items [5] = { 0, 0, 0, 0, 0 };

// In this all elements are initializes to 0;

after that we can insert element at specific index by specifying index number.

items [0] = 100;

```
items [ 1 ] = 99;
items [ 2 ] = 98;
items [ 3 ] = 97;
items [ 4 ] = 96;
```

Suppose programer needs to insert at index 80 of array of size 100 then it can shown below as,

```
items [ 80 ] = 111;
```

5.2.2 Initialisation Of Two Dimensional Array.

In example 5.1.2 can be specified below

In this all elements are initialises to 0;

```
int items [ 5 ] [ 5 ] = { { 0, 0, 0, 0, 0 },
                          { 0, 0, 0, 0, 0 },
                          { 0, 0, 0, 0, 0 },
                          { 0, 0, 0, 0, 0 },
                          { 0, 0, 0, 0, 0 } } ;
```

Suppose programer needs to insert at index 80 of array of size

[100] [100] then it can shown below as,

```
items [ 0 ] [ 80 ] = 111;
```

5.2.3 Initialization Of Multidimensional Array.

In example 5.1.3 can be specified below

In this all elements are initialise to 0;

```
int items [ 2 ] [ 2 ] [ 2 ] = { {
                                 { 0 , 0 } ,
                                 { 0 , 0 } ,
                              } ,
                                 { { 0 , 0 } ,
                                 { 0 , 0 } ,
                                   } } ;
```

Suppose programmer needs to insert at index 80 of array size [100] [100] [100] then it can be shown below as,

```
items [ 0 ] [ 0 ] [ 80 ] = 111;
```

On the same basis we can have many dimensions as required by software project specified in square bracket.

Note: In initialisation of array as an example, consider an array of size 3 x 3 indexing of array as follows,

```
int items [ 3 ] [ 3 ] = {
[ 0 ] [ 0 ], [ 0 ] [ 1 ], [ 0 ] [ 2 ],     // represent 1st row
[ 1 ] [ 0 ], [ 1 ] [ 1 ], [ 1 ] [ 2 ],     // represent 2nd row
[ 2 ] [ 0 ], [ 2 ] [ 1 ], [ 2 ] [ 2 ]      // represent 3rd row
};
```

Consider another example of 2 x 2 indexing of array as follows,

```
int items [ 2 ] [ 2 ] = {
[ 0 ] [ 0 ], [ 0 ] [ 1 ] ,                 // represent 1st row
[ 1 ] [ 0 ], [ 1 ] [ 1 ]                   // represent 2nd row
};
```

5.3 Character Array

Character array is similar to integer array in storing elements. Any array stores single element at any index in array. Since it is character array have ' char ' as a datatype hold single byte. Now all chapters of ASCII set are of single byte and Unicode characters are of two bytes say chines character set. To explain this scenario consider a home automation system in programer needs to name various programming entity to define architecture of automation system. In C there is no direct support of string type but made with character array. In C++ programmer can use string datatype as it is already supported by C++ by using " string.h " header file. Character array is null terminated array. It means that last element in array is ' \0 ' is called null character.

5.3.1 Declaration of character array

1. char itemName [31];

In above declaration, array is able to store item name of maximum length of 31 characters. It will be terminated by null character at last.

2. char itemNames [3] [31];

In above declaration, array is able to store three item name of maximum length of 31 characters. It will be terminated by null character at last.

5.3.2 Initialisation of character array

Character arrays are initialise the same way as integer array but with null termination at last.

```
char itemName [ 13 ] =

{ ' G ', ' I ', ' R ', ' I ' , ' S ' , ' H ', ' . ',
 ' S ' , ' H ' , ' E ' , ' T ' , ' Y ' ,' E ' , ' \0 ' } ;

char itemNames [ 2 ] [ 13 ] = {

                    { " GirishAjitShetye " } ,

                    { " NaviMumbaiMH " }

                         };
```

In this multiple char array is initialise.

Now if programer wants to modify a character from itemName, then it is possible by accessing index of char array as below,

```
from above example : itemName [ 2 ] = ' T ' ;

so new array becomes as below,

itemName [ 0 ] = ' G ';

itemName [ 1 ] = ' I ';

itemName [ 2 ] = ' T ';   ........ // new value

itemName [ 3 ] = ' I ';

itemName [ 4 ] = ' S ';

itemName [ 5 ] = ' H ';

itemName [ 6 ] = ' ';

itemName [ 7 ] = ' S ';

itemName [ 8 ] = ' H ';
```

```
itemName [ 9 ] = ' E ';
itemName [ 10 ] = ' T ';
itemName [ 11 ] = ' Y ';
itemName [ 12 ] = ' E ';
itemName [ 13 ] = ' \0 ';
```

5.4 Reading Character Array Dynamically

- Integer Array

Since integer array is a set of integer elements stored in memory. To access integer array of 2D needs two indexes. With use of single for loop we read only 1D array.

say I need to store size of home automation display to display various logos, images, icons to fit within display. One dimensional array and 2D array represent length and x-y coordinate system respectively. If you add 3D array then x-y-z coordinate system it represent in software application industry. 3D array are famous in CAD/CAM industry.

So, let's consider,

```
int plane[10];
```

This stores ten planes length as only it have one dimension i.e. it represent only one quantity.

```
for (int index = 0; index < 10; index++)
        scanf("%d", plane[index])
```

Similarly, in case of 2D stores,

Let's consider,

```
int plane[5][10];
```

This stores total 50 elements of five different planes, each plane have ten quantity, so total 50. It also indicate x-y coordinated planes. Or someone says area of a particular plane. Now we cannot use single index so we need two indexes to traverse 2D and three indexes to travel 3D array. 3D represent x-y-z or volumetric representation of object in software. 2D and 3D represent two and three different quantities of objects in software industry.

```
for (int index1 = 0; index1 < 5; index1++)
```

```
for (int index2 = 0; index2 < 10; index2++)
        scanf("%d", &plane[index1][index2]);
```

Similarly for 3D array

```
for (int index1 = 0; index1 < 5; index1++)
        for (int index2 = 0; index2 < 10; index2++)
        for (int index3 = 0; index3 < 10; index3++)
        scanf("%d", &plane[index1][index2][index3]);
```

- Character Array:

Character is a one byte variable. In array at any particular location only single character is stored. To store two character we need two location separately.

char name[21];

stores 20 characters inside it and null terminated.

```
scanf("%s", name)
```

So following statement reads application name upto twenty-one characters.

Similarly, char name[4][21];

```
for(int index = 0;index<=4;index++)
scanf("%s",bankAccountHolderName[index][0]);
```

So following statements read four application names of length upto twenty-one characters. Other index is always pointed to first location of each name read.

Note: Please refer chapter 13 for examples on array.

5.5 Summary

- This is very special chapter in C programming context. But the issue is that it uses continuous memory location. So when such a requirement comes into use case, we go for structures and do dynamic allocation. You will come across in upcoming chapter.
- Normally when we have develope embedded application, then memory restrictions are present because of small size of memory.
- Information that application handle is sufficiently less. The choice made by application developer is use of different types of use of arrays.

- So lots of variable declaration is not required of same type.
- Array can be integer, float, double, char type, helping in providing continuous memory allocation and it simplified operations.
- We can allocate memory ton array on heap for dynamicity, using malloc() C function.
- We have multi-dimensional array to hold multiple information of same type. Its elements are accessed by specifying its index in square brackets ([ ])

5.6 Hausaufgaben

1. Write a program to determine determinant of matrix A. Det. A = |A| for two and three dimensional matrix.
2. Find minimum and maximum number present in given list. [A] = {1,2,3,50,39,45,60,99,97,98,13}; min=1, max=99.
3. Apply Heap Sort, Selection Sort, Bubble Sort and Binary Search, Linear Search algorithm for following matrix, [A] = {1,2,3,50,39,45, 60,99,97,98,13};
4. Perform Matrix addition, subtraction and multiplication on any 3 x 3 matrix.

Refer Chapter 13 for answer.

Chapter 6.
Structure and Union in C and C++

6.1 Structure

Structure in programming languages are very useful as they are capable to hold heterogeneous information in a single block. This type of block holding different datatypes as a single unit is called structure in programming. Developer can create arrays of heterogeneous block called array of structure as it holds many entries of same info. All members of structures are public in C as there is no access specifier available like C++. In C++ structure members are private means programmer do not have direct access to data. It has to go through functions defined in public section of structure. This modified version of structure is called class in C++ but structure also supported by it. C++ structure are better versions of C structure. To explain structures in C consider a home automation system in developer needs to create many buttons for LED lights, two FANs and TV switch button. Now beginner level programmer design this by creating many LED lights, FANs and TV SWITCH button. This kind of programming took much efforts in application development as its code size grows in lines. Sometimes to create modular application suitable for further development and addition of more features in application basic techniques doesn't help. So programmer needs more sophisticated techniques to handle increase complicity. One way is use of structure in C. In C we make one single unit of LED lights, FANs and TV SWITCH rather creating on demand on application requirement by programmer. But in this case you need to create array of structure. This is similar to creation of individual elements and accessing them individually as and when required. This saves lots of programming efforts and makes it simple to write applications as it reduces complexity of development.

Syntax:

```
struct struct_name {
        datatype memberName;
        datatype memberName;
        datatype memberName;
        ...
```

```
};
```

Example:

```
struct detailPersonInfo
{
        char personFirstName [ 31 ];
        char personMiddleName [ 31 ];
        char personLastName [ 31 ];
        char personMotherName [ 31 ];
        int personAge;
        char personSex [ 12 ];
        int isGraduate;    // 0 if yes otherwise 1
};
```

6.1.1 Declaring Structure Variables

Before declaring structure variables programmer needs to define struct as mentioned in section 6.1. Now developer can define as many variables of struct type and initialise them on needed by project requirement.

Syntax:

```
struct detailPersonalInfo personInfo_1, personInfo_2, personInfo_3;
```

Many modern compiler allows to declaring structure variables without use of keyword ' struct ' as below

Syntax:

```
detailPersonalInfo personInfo_1, personInfo_2, personInfo_3;
```

6.1.2 Initialisation of Structure

Initialisation technique used for structure is called static initialisation of structure variables.

```
struct detailPersonalInfo personalInfo_1 =
                { "girish" , "ajit" , "shetye" , "hemlata" ,
                37 ,"male" , 0 };
struct detailPersonalInfo personalInfo_2 =
```

```
{ "ajit" , "nana" , "shetye" , "hemlata" ,
        62 , "male" , 1
    };
struct detailPersonalInfo personalInfo_3 =
    { "hemlata" , "ajit" , "shetye" , "girish" ,
    58 , "female" , 1
    };
```

Initialisation technique used for structure is called dynamic initialisation of structure variables.

To initialise char array we need to take help of C string API library does this task simpler. Further to access struct variable C have dot (.) operator to member variable.

Example:

```
strcpy ( personalInfo_1.personFirstName , "devdasnath" );
strcpy(personalInfo_1.personMiddleName , "dasramnath");
strcpy ( personalInfo_1.personLastName , "yadavnath" );
strcpy (personalInfo_1.personMotherName , "hemanath" );
personalInfo_1.personAge = 37;
strcpy ( personalInfo_1.personSex , "female" );
personalInfo_1.isGraduate = 1;
```

6.1.3 Rules for Initialisation Of Structure

1. Uninitialise structure members are assigns default values zero for integers and floating point numbers , ' \0 ' for characters and strings.
2. Initialisation must be done in order.
3. We can not initialise structure member inside declaration.

6.1.4 Memory Allocation for Structure.

In structure memory is allocated to each variable based on its datatype. Since structure is of heterogeneous type allocation is not uniform. To prevent comparison from entering garbage entries, structure members are kept one byte align from each datatype. So this byte is called slack byte in structure. This byte is filled with garbage information resulting into change in the size of structure or varies on system use.

Example.

1st Byte	Slack Byte	2nd Byte	
'D'	Garbage Byte	1	2

In example, 1st byte holds character after that slack byte and 2nd byte holds integer value of 2 bytes. Slack byte content is not known to programer as he do not have access to it. It is internally handled by OS for allocation in memory on stack.

6.1.5 Other possible implementation with structures are

1. Array of structure
2. Array within structure
3. Structure within structure

A developer must be smart enough for explore above implementations as basics given with proper and practical home automation implementation scenario.

6.2 Union

Unions are same as structure but with only difference is that one memory allocations. Union also made of heterogeneous types, but as a structure memory allocation is done for each individual member not in case of union. In case of union memory allocation is done only for member of largest storage requirement. Other members are using same storage on requirement. Previous information stored in this storage is overwritten by new record. To explain this scenario consider a situation of designing of embedded hardware have limited memory requirement example loading boot loader program used to initialise OS in computer. Another example of automatic washing machine have limited resource and must be use to save cost of H/S development.

Syntax:

```
union unionName {
        datatype memberName;
        datatype memberName;
};
```

Example:

```
union initHardware {
        int hardwareAddress;
        char startBootP;
};
```

6.2.1 Declaration of Union members

Before use of union variable, union must be define along with proper members. Now developer can define as many variables of union type and initialise them on needed by project requirement. Dot (.) operator is used to access union members.

Syntax:

```
union unionName unionVariable1, unionVariable2;
```

Example:

```
union initHW initHW1, initHW2;
```

6.2.2 Initialisation of Union

Initialisation of union is done the same way as it done for structure. Union member be initialise below:

initHW1.hwAddress = 2009;

initHW1.startBootP = ' A '; // after initialisation old value 2009 replace by new value ' A '.

6.3 Bit Fields

Bit fields are used to set individual bits of memory of application as specially in embedded systems by application programmer. To explain this scenario consider home automation system. Customer needs to turn on LED lights in room. To on lights hardware bit must be set to logic HIGH level. To accomplish setting bit provision IC designer provides libraries. With help of library API developer set bit in hardware and LED lights in room gets ON. In similar way LED lights in room gets OFF. To achieve functionality of setting bits in embedded application bit fields are very very useful. Each bit can be configured as per requirement by the developer of embedded application.

Developer specifies allocation of bits useful in particular case. In a LED lights ON / OFF user needs to turn on individual LED light or in groups. So in particular room six (6) LED lights are present, developer can reserved eight (8) bits or I mean one complete byte and use only six (6) bit out of eight (8) bits. This saves application memory allocation requirement by developer. In this developer can assign each bit to individual part or group individual bits say two (2) each to turn ON / OFF two LED lights together by customer.

Syntax:

```
struct variable_name {
        datatype variableName : bitLenght;
        datatype variableName : bitLenght;
        datatype variableName : bitLenght;
        datatype variableName : bitLenght;
        datatype variableName : bitLenght;
};
```

Example:

```
struct led_Lights {
        unsigned int ledLight1 : 1;
        unsigned int ledLight2 : 1;
        unsigned int ledLight34 : 2;
        unsigned int ledLight5 : 1;
        unsigned int ledLight67 : 2;
        unsigned int ledLight8 : 1;
} lights;
```

This defines variable field name lights with seven bit fields. Range could be depends on number of bits assigns to each bit fields. Each bit holds two values either one or zero. Depending on size of bits assigns for example two bits gives four combinations and so on.

1. The first field always starts with first bit of the word.
2. The length of all the fields in structure should not be more than size of word. Overlapping fields are automatically forced to beginning of the next word.

3. Datatype is either int or unsigned int or signed int. Signed bit field must be of 2 bits minimum.
4. We can not access bit fields by its address.
5. Bit fields can not be arrayed.

6.3.1 Initialisation Of Bit Fields

```
lights.ledLight1 = 0;      // led light ON
lights.ledLight1 = 1;      // led light OFF
lights.ledLight67 =  3;    //led light 6 and 7 both are OFF
lights.ledLight67 = 2;     //led light 6 and 7 both are ON
```

Example:

Above mentioned "led_Lights" structure of bit filed size is calculated as,

printf("Size Of led_lights Structure Is = %lu \n",sizeof(struct led_Lights));

Size Of led_lights Structure Is = 4 bytes

Now if we run same example by removing individual bit fields mention, the output of space occupied by structure field as a whole is mentioned below,

printf("Size Of led_lights Structure Is = %lu \n",sizeof(struct led_Lights));

Size Of led_lights Structure Is = 24 bytes

as unsigned int occupies 4 bytes each member.

so we saves around 20bytes of memory with the help of bit fields. Lets say a programmer wants to communicates with small memory device like washing machine controller, a developer must use bit fields as limitedness of space required by application. So it becomes cost, space and performance wise effective too.

6.4 Summary

- This chapter speaks about structure, unions and bit-fields. They are essential component and basic need of application development.
- Now, structure can be used to hold heterogeneous information as a single unit of data encapsulation.
- In large application such as banking app, lots of customer related information as well as his account related information is to be process

and must relate to customer account. It must be valid information. The only way we have in C is to use structure and in C++ we have classes.

- So by referring structure variable, we can access customer info. So burden of having millions customer variables and variables tracking in application become cumbersome task.
- One mistake to hold wrong balance info will be mess in case of banking application. Debugging of such a application is tiresome task for developer.
- We can access structure member by (.) dot operator, in case of static linking and by arrow (→) operator.
- As stack is limited we can perform dynamic linking by using malloc and calloc and realloc library functions.
- Coming to next is union. Unions are same as structure with largest size allocation as a whole. Individual members cannot participate in separate memory block allocation.
- Union have to use existing memory block with largest size allocated by malloc on heap. So union will hold size with largest memory required by mention variable.
- Once used for allocation previous info is not available with that memory variable.
- This kind of use of union is made in embedded application development where memory is of few Byte or Kbyte.
- Bit-fields are allocating specific bit to a particular variable in bit-fields. I can allocate 4-bits to hold lower nipple and 3-bits to hold country code and assign one bit to on/off LED lights.
- So using bit-fields, we can assign individual bit operation on user information. Example ti insert/eject ATM card.

6.5 Hausaufgaben

1. Write a program to control stepper motor such that by pressing a switch on board that changes the direction of motor rotation. By pressing off key it stops rotation of motor.
2. Write a program to scroll message "Jai Hind, Jai Bharat" on LCD/LED panel available with Arduino/Raspberry PI board.

3. Write a program to have personal info form to open a account in bank. Once customer information is available perform bank transaction such as transfer bank from one account to another account in different bank. Disable account and disable specific feature of account.
4. Write a program to glow LED red in colour and other LED yellow in colour. On button press they should swap their colour.

NOTES

Chapter 7.
Functions in C and C++

Functions in C and C++ are very important aspects of programming languages. These technique of writing application reduce considerable development work and make application writing very easy for development work. To explain this scenario consider home automation system in that programmer have one task to be repeatedly called like ON and OFF of different systems connected home automation i.e. LED, FAN, TV and many more. Now to achieve this task programmer needs to called ON and OFF several times in each place. This increases number of lines of code since such a code need to be called at several places. It is also very difficult to debug code called at several places for same purpose. To achieve and facilitates professional coding practices is to code once and called several times with the help of functions. In this case there will be two functions ON and OFF with desired parameter full filing functional specifications. To achieve this in programming language like C and C++ functions where introduce. They helps in modular programming by dividing complete programer into individual units for better implementation for team. The basic difference between C and C++ functions is they support function overloading and overriding as these features are not available in C functions.

7.1 Function Definition

Syntax:

```
return_type function_name ( datatype argument1,
                            datatype argument2, ... )
{
        //statements of functions
        return return_value;
}
```

Example1:

```
int turnONLights ( light ledON ) {
        switchONLight ( ledON );
```

```
        return 1;
}
```

Example2:

```
int turnOFFLights ( light ledOFF ) {
        switchOFFLight ( ledOFF );
        return 0;
}
```

7.2 Function consist of following parts

1. return type
2. function name
3. function arguments
4. function statements in body
5. return value based on return type specified
6. function also have prototype defined before having function body.
7. if no return type is specified then in place of return type ‘ void ‘ keyword is used indicating there is no return type for function.
8. if no argument is specified in function then ‘ void ‘ is specified as a argument.

7.3 Function prototype

Function prototype is used before function body. It tells compiler that such a function name exist with given arguments and return type i.e.

Syntax:

```
return_type function_name ( datatype argument1, datatype
        argument2, . . . );
```

7.4 Function Call

Function call is a statement in programming language used to invoke function from this control is transferred function definition in memory. From memory code is loaded into application memory and gets executed to perform specified task.

Syntax:

```
function_name ( argument1, argument2, .. );
```

Example1:

```
turnONLights ( ledON );
```

Example2:

```
turnOFFLights ( ledOFF );
```

7.5 Passing different types of data to function

1. Built-in Type
2. User define Type
3. Unions

7.5.1 Built-in types are called primitive datatypes are passed to function as below

```
return_type function_name ( int/float/char  variable_name );
return_type function_name ( int/float/char  variable_name )
        {
                // statements;
        }
        function_name ( variable_name );
```

7.5.2 User-defined types comes under are array, structure.

Consider passing array elements to function:

```
        int items [ 4 ] = { 1, 2, 3, 4 };
void itemsToSell ( int items [ 4 ] );
void itemsToSell ( int items [ 4 ] ) {
                // statements;
        }
        itemsToSell ( items );
```

Consider passing structure to function:

```
struct itemsHomeAutomation items =
        { LED_ON, LED_OFF, "MySweetHome", 37 };
void itemsOfHomeAutomation ( struct
itemsHomeAutomation items );
void itemsOfHomeAutomation ( struct
itemsHomeAutomation items ) {
        // statements;
}
itemsOfHomeAutomation ( items );
```

7.6 Recursive Function In C and C++

In C++ function is of ordinary type and recursive type. Ordinary type have call on stack do not have multiple stack unwinding. It have only single return value with single entry on stack. But in case of recursive call there will be multiple entry on same stack address.

In recursive function (RF) call function will be called inside same function with return value as a statement. This function when called in reverse order that is final value gets called first on recursion, and then subsequent call to return final value of execution is made by function. Function with this kind of function call stack unwinding on same address is called recursive function. In recursive function is called inside same function with return value is called RF.

Syntax:

```
return-type functionName (data-type argument-passed) {
        return functionName (data-type argument-passed)
}
```

Example:

```
int calculateFactorial(int number) {
if(number == 0)
        return 1;
else
```

```
        return number * calculateFactorial(number-1)
    }
```

In the above example, factorial of 5 is calculated by recursive method output to 120 in number. In calculation calculateFactorial() is called inside factorial function and function is exited by unwinding last to first stack value as shown below,

5 * calculateFactorial (5 - 1)

5 * 4 calculateFactorial (4 - 1) ~ 20 * calculateFactorial (4 - 1)

20 * 3 calculateFactorial (3 - 1) ~ 60 * calculateFactorial (3 - 1)

60 * 2 calculateFactorial (2 - 1) ~ 120 * calculateFactorial (2 - 1)

120 * 1 = 120.

So final answer is 120.

7.7 Summary

- This chapter explains about functions and their use. With this feature unorganized code becomes organized and modular one.
- Modular one means we can create or bundle useful and reusable work as a separate module. We can store modules into memory and use whenever required by app developer.
- Because C uses function for modular programming that's why C is called or famous for modular programming App development.
- These function/modular blocks of code as capable of returning result of their operation and do further processing.

7.8 Hausaufgaben

1. Write a program for factorial of a number by using factorial function to calculate factorial.
2. Write a program to calculate even and odd series by using functions.
3. Write a program to calculate binomial expression. Use functions.
4. Write a program to calculate area, volume and perimeter of different types of triangle. Use functions to define modules.

NOTES

Chapter 8.

Pointers in C and C++

8.1 Introduction to Pointers in C and C++

Pointers in C and C++ are similar but the there is no concept of objects in C, they are limited to primitives and user defined types such as arrays and structures. Use of pointers are very helpful allocating memory on heap. Heap memory is a memory other than stack memory. Whenever programer use variables without memory allocation then memory will be allocated on stack and allocation is temporary but with memory allocation it will be on heap until deleted by programmer manually in application development. Stack is limited in application as it doesn't required to be more for allocation since temporary storage which is sufficient. But heap size needs to be maximum as allocating data permanently during execution of programme. Application required to access data or information stored during lifecycle of application. Customer calls various services given by application. In this process if information is stored on stack then it become unavailable to application because its temporary but this is not case with heap. To explain this scenario with consider a configuration files loaded by application in stack memory, now in modular programming technique once scope of particular modules exit then data in memory is unavailable. So to solve this developer required heap memory allocation. This memory is available until explicitly deleted during application by calling ' free () ' in C or ' delete ' in case of C++. Heap is bigger in size than stack memory because of above scenario.

Syntax:

```
datatype *pionter_variable;
```

Example.

```
int id = 6;        //declaration of non pointer variable
int *prtId;        //declaration of pointer variable with help of asterisk (
* )
ptrId = &id;       //initialisation of pointer variable.
```

id prtId ptrId = &id

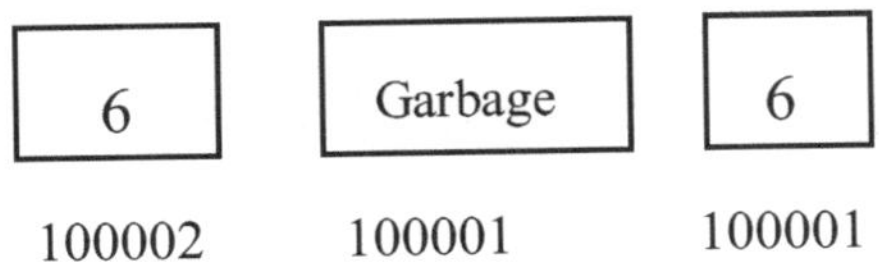

In above scenario variable ' id ' holds value. ptrId holds pointer variable at address 100001 pointing to garbage value. After declaration of pointer variable, it mades to point 100002 memory address holding six (6) as a value at address 100001. So programmer make use of pointer to point another variable in memory.

Initialisation of pointer is done only through assignment of reference. Following assignment is illegal in C and C++;

```
char *ptr;
*ptr = "wrong initialisation";        // generates compilation error
printf("%s",*ptr);
```

8.1.2 Pointer technique

In using pointer contains two steps of accessing data. In first pointer variable needs to be made pointing to data variable using ' reference ' operator (&) and value present at address is access by using asterisk operator (*). This is called de-referencing of pointers.

1. Reference of pointer means pointing to address of variable its pointing.

2. De-Referencing of pointer means pointing to value of variable its pointing.

8.1.3 Rules of pointer operations

1. A pointer variable can be used to hold address of another variable i.e. programmer assigns pointer variable address.
2. Assigns value to another variable
3. A pointer can be initialised with NULL or unique value.
4. Pointer variable can be incremented or decremented by one.
5. Integer value can be added or subtracted from pointer variable.
6. A pointer variable cannot be multiplied by constant.
7. We cannot add multiple pointer variables.

8. A value cannot be assigned to an arbitrary address (&ptr = 10; is illegal)

8.2 Important about pointers

Pointer is incremented or decremented on the size of datatype. To explain this scenario consider a character pointer of 1 byte. If we increment character pointer then it will always incremented by one. So on similar basis if we increment integer pointer it gets incremented by four and same with other datatypes. Size of datatype depends on compiler as well as processor used for application development.

Following example.

char = 1 byte always irrespective of platform

integer = 4 bytes platform specific

float = 4 bytes platform specific

double = 8 bytes platform specific

8.3 Pointers with functions

Pointers are very helpful in allocating data on heap memory. To allocate data multiple times on heap memory developer needs a common method which does the task of allocation. When we use modules, we need to pass information. Passing of information with help of functions with pointers as a argument.

There are two techniques followed to pass arguments to function by using pointers.

8.3.1 Call By Value.

In call by value technique original variable value doesn't get modified even after modification inside function. This technique of passing copy of a value to function is called call by value.

8.3.2 Call By Reference.

In call by reference technique, reference of original value is passed to function with reference technique resulted into modification of original value if modified inside function. This technique of passing reference of original value if any modification results into new value in original value know as call by reference. amp (&).

Example:

```
void changeMyRecord ( int *ptrRecord );
void changeMyRecord ( int *ptrRecord ) {
        // statements
        *ptrRecord = 4;
}
int ptr  =  5;
changeMyRecord ( &ptr );
```

Example:

```
void swapNumbers(int *num1,int *num2) {
int temp;
temp = *num1;
*num1 = *num2;
*num2 = temp;
}
```

8.4 Pointer to Functions

A pointer to function is a technique of calling function with the help of pointers. In case of non pointer function it is an ordinary function call. This ordinary function call will have stack entry during execution and it will wind in the way stack design. Design of stack have bottom-up and top-down approach of winding stack. So it requires lots stack handling efforts. It is time consuming in the sense of stack unwinding speed. But with help of function pointer also called pointer to function speed of execution of function call speed increases to great extent since stack unwinding is not required. Function call will be directly replaced from call from memory allocated to function. To explain this scenario consider that customer needs to SWITCH ON / OFF led lights. Now switching ON/OFF led requires fast response. To meet this requirement software used for operating led requires fast response. To achieve fast response developer needs to increase execution speed of software with the help of pointer to function also called as function pointers.

Declaration:

```
return-datatype ( * functionpointer ) ( datatype argument1,
        datatype argument2, … );
```

Initialisation of function pointer:

```
functionpointer = functionName;
```

Call to function pointer:

```
( * functionpointer ) ( value1, value2, … );
```

Example:

1. Declaration of function pointer with no arguments

```
int ( * functionIntegerPointer ) ( );
```

2. Assignment of address of function called

```
functionIntegerPointer = getIntegerValue;
```

3. Call to function using function pointer

```
( * functionIntegerPointer ) ( );
```

Example:

In following example a wrapper is written to call function with argument. Wrapper function accept one argument as a function pointer and another is ordinary integer argument. In which same function wrapper is used to call two different function to glow LEDS of regulator and fan.

```
#include <stdio.h>
void OnFanLEDNo(int lNum) {
        printf("Fan With LED No %d Is ON.\n",lNum);
}
void OnRegulatorLED(int lRegNum) {
        printf("Regulator LED No %d Is ON.\n",lRegNum);
}
void abstractionToFunCall(void (*abstraction)(int lNo),int lNum) {
        (*abstraction)(lNum); // function call using wrapper function
}
int main() {
        abstractionToFunCall(OnFanLEDNo,4);
        abstractionToFunCall(OnRegulatorLED,5);
```

```
        // code added for array of function pointer using subscript   operator [ ]
        void (*hideCall[])(int) = {  OnRegulatorLED,
                                       OnFanLEDNo
                                    };
        (*hideCall[0])(10);
        (*hideCall[1])(10);
        return 0;
}
```

Output:

```
        Fan With LED No 4 Is ON.
        Regulator LED No 5 Is ON.
        Regulator LED No 10 Is ON.
        Fan With LED No 10 Is ON.
```

8.5 Summary

- This chapter introduces pointers and its use. Whenever information is copied we use variables. But them how we copy information from heap memory rather than stack memory.
- Solution is to use pointers. Pointer allows interfacing different communication device to computer or any embedded hardware.
- We can send and receive info from communicating device such as USB, UART etc. It also required baud rate to match.
- Allows copying information heap memory to cache memory. As we limited stack memory.

8.6 Hausaufgaben

1. Write a program copy data from heap memory to a stack memory.
2. Write a program to copy one 3 x 3 matrix from heap to stack by using pointers. i.e. copy one matrix to another one with help of pointers only.
3. Perform pointer arithmetic such as addition, subtraction and multiplication on pointer type info.

Chapter 9.

File Handling In C.

Introduction

File handling in C is quite bit older technique used for configuration of application and storage of records inserted during application execution. Nowadays database programming is available to hold increase demand of storage information that may be available in different formats. e.g. image, audio, video, audio video, textual, time etc. To explain this scenario consider a home automation system in service provider required billing details unit about usage, to display percentage usage of consumption, fan speed and other configurations over UI and to keep updated configuration file for internal reference for backup, in case of restart to load configuration i.e. original settings in case of boot loader. Another example I can share with you is cloud logging data embedded system. One example is of Facebook to store user information required by Facebook in remote or local server over internet protocol. To store large information large storage servers are required. File handling in C is provides many in-built APIs to facilitates file handling functions.

9.1 File Handling Operations

1. Console Related I/O Operations.
2. File Related Operations

To handle console related I/O operations by programmer there is ' scanf ' and ' printf ' functions are available doing read and write functionality. On the same basis to perform file related operation many APIs are available for different types of file format.

Basic APIs used during file oerations in C and C++

File Handling APIs	Operations Performed By APIs
FILE* fopen (const char *restrict filename, const char *restrict mode)	Creates a new file for use. Opens an existing for use
int fclose (FILE* fpointer)	Closes a file which has been opened for use
int getc (FILE* fpointer)	Reads a character from file

int putc (int c, FILE* fpointer)	Writes a character to a file
int fprintf (FILE * restrict fpointer, const char * restrict format, ...)	Writes a set of data values to a file
int fscanf (FILE *restrict fpointer, const char *restrict format, ...)	Reads a set of data values from a file
int getw (FILE* fpointer)	Reads an integer to a file
int putw (int w, FILE* fpointer)	Writes an integer to a file
int (FILE *fpointer, long offset, int whence)	Sets the position to a desired point in the file.
long ftell (FILE *fpointer)	Gives the current position in file
void rewind (FILE *fpointer)	Sets the position to the beginning of the file

Notes: After completing file handling related operations file pointer must be closed and pointer must be freed from containing any memory information.

Refer chapter 13.4 for a file handling example.

Example related to file handling must be practice by own, say read single file and break it into two files of size 1KB and another is remaining KB.

9.2 File Handling Modes

"r" stands for read operation on existing file. On successful opening of file returns pointer to 1st character. On failure returns NULL.

"w" stands for write operation on file. File content is overriding existing file. If file is not present on media, it creates file.

"a" stands for append mode on existing file. File pointer points to last character on opening file. Content is appended at the end of file.

"+" is used to combine file operation on file. Suppose application needs read , write operation together then with "r+a" programmer can read and write to file say database file used in banking app on mobile phones. Database file also required append operation so use append mode. New record is always inserted at end of last character on opening a file.

All "r", "w", "a" returns NULL of failure of file open i.e fopen() operations.

Note: Refer Chapter 13 for example. Logger Example.

Summary

- In this chapter we talk about file handling and API used for file handling.
- To work with files we need to first open the file by using FILE * pointer variable. Once we locate the file in memory, user can perform various operations on file.
- A good example is EXCEL sheets used Manager to perform asset related information. Finance related info or accounts related calculations are stored in a file.
- In older day, when initial development information is stored in file. Now a day's server dependent and independent database files are used to hold big information.
- Cloud computing is one of latest technology to store user as well as application specific in remote server. It process lots of data i.e. Big Data

Hausaufgaben

1. Refer chapter 13 for file handling info. Logger logs application logs. When we analyze logger file come to know what happen to application during crash.
2. By writing customer info into customer.info file demonstrate banking application. Also add authentication related info before opening a file.

NOTES

Chapter 10.
String API.

10.1 Introduction

String APIs are already developed libraries that are readily available for development of application. API is a function developed by some developer on specific platform. Made available to developer to write application with help of existing functionalities. So job of application developer is to just include APIs header file and use API provided or written by some other developer. Suppose, an calculator application needs to do lots of mathematical calculations. So to develop application or used pre-available functionality of maths to be used so no need to write mathematical calculations again to develop or new calculator application. Or another example is printf() and scanf() functions. These API are already available in package form. Similarly to perform basic staring related operations string APIs are already developed and readily used in by developer to reduce rewriting same functionality for individual application. In one line these are pre-built libraries used by application developer to develop application on specific or common platform. Many developer usually called them "intellectual-property" and if used needs developing organization permission. For specific or common hardware core these libraries are designed.

String APIs plays important role in programming language. They are high level languages meaning easy to read by humans for interaction with hardware. Humans are unable to know hardware but with help of string APIs customer interact with UI by digitally given interface. To explain this scenario consider a home automation system in customer needs to interact with digital interface. But humans unable to know internal details if given for interaction on UI. To solve this interface issue developer use string handling APIs.

String API are very useful in console application. Messages are used to inform or make aware what action to select to perform which action. Now a day's best example is of banks ATM machines. Customer interact with most simple UI made of buttons containing string messages and user also notifies successful or failure of operation by customer transaction.

Strings are basically high-level human readable words helping in SMS messages by a telecom operators. With string containing application can alert weather, medical messages to doctors, about patient condition, whatsapp chat messages, email communication. Strings are very helpful in messaging app, to search a particular topic in google website, to give details of product on product website, to online eduction websites, to payment and shopping websites and apps in mobile phones and so on strings are helpful and useful in programming world. No application are made without strings and string APIs.

To work with string related operation programmer must include "<string.h>" header file. To handle C strings use character array of specific length.

10.2 Basic APIs used during file operations in C and C++

String Handling APIs	Operations performed by APIs
char* strcat (char *restrict ,const char *restrict)	Concatenates two strings
int strcmp (const char *, const char *)	Compares two strings
char* strcpy (char *dest, const char *src)	Copies string into original string
size_t strlen (const char *)	Calculates number of character
char* strncpy(char *dest, const char *src, size_t)	Copies n number of character into original string
int strncmp (const char *, const char *, size_t)	Compares n number of character with original string
strncat (char *restrict, const char *restrict, size_t)	Concatenates n character with original string
char *strstr (const char *big, const char *little)	Finds string mentioned in original string
size_t strnlen(const char *, size_t maxlen)	Calculates number of characters upto maximum length
char *strnstr (const char *big, const char *little,size_t)	Finds string mentioned in original string upto size n

Refer example in Chapter 13.8 example for string API "strcmp".

10.3 Summary

- Strings are very important set of characters array terminated by null character. '\0' is called null character value in C.
- If any character array found containing null value, considered to be terminated and subsequent values are not read by application.

- %s format specifier is used to read character collectively up to null terminated character.

10.4 Hausaufgaben

3. Find length of string using C.
4. Concatenate string a1 = “Navi Mumbai” and string a2 = “Kharghar” to produce third string a3 = “Kharghar, Navi Mumbai.” In a3 add “,” and “.” as shown in string a3.
5. Find frequency of input character in given string. Also reverse the assume string that you considered.
6. Implement string functions without help of string library functions. E.g. strcat, remove(int index, char ch) etc.

NOTES

Chapter 11.
Dynamic Memory Management and Linked List

Introduction

In programming language two major types of memory allocation available. One is allocation on stack and other on heap. Allocation on stack is done automatically and it is temporary but allocation on heap is a manual process and permanent until freed manually. To avail permanent allocation on heap programming APIs are available easing task of heap allocation. This topic is very well explained .

11.1 Basic APIs used during dynamic memory allocation

Dynamic Memory Allocation APIs	Operation performed by APIs
void* malloc (size_t)	Allocates request size of bytes and returns a pointer to the first byte of the allocated space.
void* calloc (size_t , size_t)	Allocates Space for an array of elements, initializes them to zero and then returns a pointer to memory.
void free(void *)	Frees Previously Allocated Space
void* realloc(void *,size_t)	Modifies the size of previously allocated space

Notes: Header file used for dynamic memory allocation handling APIs is "stdlib.h"

Example related to dynamic memory allocation must be practice by own or please contact expert in DMA technique in programming.

11.2 Linked List

Linked list is a technique of information stored in memory and connecting this information to other memory locations at random places in memory. These are heterogeneous allocation in memory i.e. no continuous allocation in memory for information stored. This linked list is always on heap segment of memory. To implement linked list developer needs to take the help of pointers and malloc memory allocation on heap function call. To integrate more information related to user for storage developer required structure so that integration will be easy with different types of information. But linked list is a technique to allocates in heap memory. Now a days database is available to store maximum information on local or remote server within country or any foreign nations over internet service. Linked list is a technique of organization of information in heap memory. Other than heap hard disk used for memory allocation as some space is reserved for dynamic memory allocation in case of insufficient memory.

Notes: Example related to Dynamic Memory Allocation (DMA) and linked list must be practice by own.

Example: Refer Section 13.6

In linked-list we use structure in C and Classes in C++. Linked-list is a structure that points to itself with new memory location on heap. This allows allocation of memory other than stack by programmer as huge requirement. One best example is of paging technique that whole chunk of memory is divided into smaller chunks and allow other application to use available free memory. Describe linked list is out of scope of this book as it is a separate topic.

```
struct Memory {
        void *ptrContent;
        struct Memory *nextMemoryBlock;
        // self referencing pointer to struct member points to next      address
}
```

11.2 Void Pointer (Void *)

In usual case pointer job is to point memory location and stored information at that location in memory. Another is to point another memory address from that location to track information or to point another single or multiple data in the form of structure or class in case of C and C++. As C is not strict about data types but C++ is.

Now void pointer (void *) is very much useful in converting sensor information to particular type in C. To explain this scenario consider a analog sensor sensing temperature in home automation system is in the form of raw data say in void pointer form because of sensor type to give in raw form. So function used in reading sensor info gives information or return in the form of void pointers as we see in case of malloc, calloc and realloc functions. But our application required to process in particular or specific type. We need to type cast info say in integer or float form. So we required a memory pointer that can be points to any type and can converted to desired form in application. Void pointer is good option available to programmer.

In memory, different type of information is stored and read from memory. To make memory information processing we need void pointer rather a specific type pointer. A good example is a reading room temperature, converting it to fahrenheit or celsius and shown on monitoring device.

Since in C, converting from void pointer to any primitive pointer type-cast is required and later this is cast to specific type info say int.

Example:

```
specific type pointer say (int *)

int *ptrTemperature = (int *) getSensorTemperature();

int mTemperature = *ptrTemperature;

void *getSensorTemperature();    // function prototype.

void *getSensorTemperature() {

        void *lPtr;          //process pointer here.

         //Only pointer declaration is mention to understand

        lPtr = malloc(10);

        // 10 bytes of memory is allocated by malloc

        return lPtr ;

}
```

In above example, getSensorTemperature() function returns void pointer and converted to integer value as mentioned.

In C++, int *ptrTemperature = getSensorTemperature(); gives error as strict to data specific conversion rules.

Note: Refer chapter 13 for example

11.3 Summary

- In dynamic memory management developer allocates memory at runtime using malloc function. So basically dynamic allocation of memory on heap is called dynamic memory allocation and its management.
- Actually OS will manage related work
- Free is use to free memory spaces allocated by malloc during its operation.

11.4 Hausaufgaben

1. State the basic difference between memory allocation functions, malloc, calloc and realloc.
2. What is the difference between free() API and delete operator.
3. Explain void * pointer. Explain "this" pointer. State the difference. And where is used practically.

Chapter 12.
The Preprocessor

The preprocessor is a technique to avoid compiler issues. In many cases with developer illiterate methods used for programming or improper architecture or not using correct standard technique specified for programming results into compiler issues. These programming issues resulted into improper functioning of binary generated. To suppress issues or warning generated by compiler stating compilers rules are not followed developer needs help of preprocessor directive to redirect these issues with the help of preprocessors. Preprocessor is specified with ' # '.

12.1 Basic Preprocessor Available in C and C++

Preprocessor Directive	Preprocessor Directive Functionality
#define	Defines a macro substitution
#undef	Un-defines a macro
#include	Specifies the files to be included
#ifdef	Test for a macro definition
#endif	Specifies the end
#ifndef	Test whether a macro is not defined
#if	Test a compiler time condition
#else	Specifies alternatives when if test fails
#elif	Sub condition in macro #if

12.2 Types of preprocessors

1. Macro Substitution preprocessors
2. File Inclusion preprocessors
3. Compiler control preprocessors

1. Macro Substitution preprocessors

Macro substitution preprocessor is a technique used in programming to hold universal constant in programming language that later expanded by compiler is called macro substitution in programming language. These macros are very helpful in faster expansion of constant and used once in programme. Changes made by macro substitution will be reflected in entire programme. It have greater maintainability effect on code. Macro substitution is used at once for only one definition of macro substitution. For each macro substitution new macro is used. Programmer can not use multiple macro substitution for single constant.

Syntax:

```
#define MACRONAME constant/expression
#define  MACRONAME “string”
```

2. File Inclusion Statements

File inclusion statements are used to include files are available outside your current scope by specifying path at location present or present at current location or from standard system inclusion path. Same directive statement used for mentioned purpose in statement. This directive is called file inclusion directive or statement normally used inside inclusive file to include file.

Syntax:

```
#include “ path / filename.ext ”  // used for non-standard path
#include “ filename.ext ” // present path is in current in file
  // present
#include <filename.ext>     // Standard library path
```

Example:

```
#include “c:/programfiles/cpp/myfavoritefilename.c” // on windows
#include “myfavoritefilename.c”
#include <stdio.h>
#include <stdlib.h>
#include <math.h>
```

3. Compiler Control Statements

Compiler directive are used to control compiler output in many embedded programming scenario. To explain this scenario consider a example of washing machine where needs to control some features and suppress warnings generated by compilers. In many cases complete features of compilers are not required or even not required by application or embedded system. To suppress or use specific features of compiler programmer needs compiler control statements or directive.

Example is math library is required so programmer includes math library by using specific statement that controls compiler and ignores rest compiler since can be used for another embedded project under consideration.

Example:

1. #pragma directive is used to specify instruction specific to compiler.

   #pragma once, warn, startup, exit, GCC, message are few examples

2. #error halt compilation process when error generates.

```
#define HEADER_FILE_MISSING
        // if commented generates error message
#ifndef HEADER_FILE_MISSING        // generates no error
#error __FILE__ IS_MISSING
#endif
```

3. Again to specify platform specific code. For example when today in market there are multiple OS are available. Now to develop application which works on multiple OS e.g. MAC OS X, LINUX, WINDOWS, SOLARIS, ANDROID, IOS. Now these OS have MACRO specific to their platforms to have platform specific code.

   1. MAC OS have "_ _Apple_ _"
   2. LINUX OS have "_ _linux_ _"
   3. WINDOWS OS have "_ _WIN32_ _"

Within this macro developer can specify there platform specific code to have cross platform application. So,

Example:

This is used in case of header file inclusion in C and C++.

```
#ifndef HEADER_FILE_NAME_H
#define HEADER_FILE_NAME_H
#include "NameOfFileToBeIncluded.h"
....
#endif //indicates end of header file
```

Example:

```
#ifdef __Apple__
// MAC OS Related Code Snippet
#endif   // end of macro definition
```

Example:

```
#if WINDOWS
        // windows related code snippet
#endif
```

12.3 Expansion OF MACROS

```
#define Add(a,b) a+b
int main() {
        printf("%d\n",Add(5,10));
        return 0;
}
```

Example:

In the below example Macro expansion took place as a expression like (a+b/a-b). So we get output as 1.000 with mention ingredients.

But if we define macro as, #define Add(a,b) (a+b) and

#define Sub(a,b) (a-b) the output will be 3.000

```
#define Add(a,b) a+b
#define Sub(a,b) a-b
int main() {
        printf("Addition Using Macro Add %d\n",Add(5,10));
        printf("Addition Using Macro Add %d\n",Sub(5,10));
        float div = 0;
        div = Add(5,10)/Sub(10,5); //expanded as (a+b/a-b)
        printf("Addition Using Macro Add %f\n",div);
return 0;
```

}

Output: 1.000

Now try same example by writing macro as said in explanation.

Macro definitions are expanded in line as mentioned and not individual macro definitions.

12.4 Summary

- In this chapter we discuss importance of preprocessor that are very helpful in writing platform specific code.
- There are three types of macros used in application development. One is to include header file required to include precompiled header APIs.
- Other one is used to differentiate platform specific code as an example in window we have Dot Net APIs. Now if we move from windows to Mac OS, dot net API doesn't work. It is needed to replace dot net API with equivalent API from Mac OS. So we use macros to separate this situation.
- Third use case is of assigning expression to the macros for fast execution of code. With macro substitution of expression have great effect on execution of code.

12.5 Hausaufgaben

1. Write a code snippet to allocate memory and free memory using C and C++. If we C code on windows then on Mac OS use C++ code. Also use appropriate header file inclusion for C and C++ if required.

NOTES

Chapter 13.
Basic Examples on C.

This chapter is fully dedicated to explain concept of C with Examples.

Example 13.1

Bubble Sort Method of Sorting Elements in Array in C

```
#include <stdio.h>
#include <stdlib.h>
void swap(int *num1,int *num2) {
  int temp;
  temp = *num1;
  *num1 = *num2;
  *num2 = temp;
}
void bublesort(int list[], int size) {
  int i,j;
  for(i=0;i<(size-1);i++)
    for(j=0;j<(size-(i+1));j++)
         if(list[j] > list[j+1])
              swap(&list[j],&list[j+1]);
}
void printlist(int list[],int size) {
  int i;
  for(i=0;i<size;i++)
    printf("%d\t",list[i]);
  printf("\n");
```

```
}
int main() {
  const int MAX_ELEMENTS_SIZE = 10;
  int list[MAX_ELEMENTS_SIZE];
  int i = 0;
  // generate random numbers and fill them to the list
  for(i = 0; i < MAX_ELEMENTS_SIZE; i++ ) {
            list[i] = rand()%100;
  }
  printf("The list before sorting is:\n");
  printlist(list,MAX_ELEMENTS_SIZE);
  bublesort(list,MAX_ELEMENTS_SIZE);    // sort the list
  // print the result
  printf("The list after sorting using bubble sorting algorithm:\n");
  printlist(list,MAX_ELEMENTS_SIZE);
  return 0;
}
```

Output 13.1

```
The list before sorting is:
7       49      73      58      30      72      44      78      23      9

The list after sorting using bubble sorting algorithm:
7       9       23      30      44      49      58      72      73      78
```

Example 13.2

Selection Sort Method of Sorting Elements in Array in C.

```
#include<stdio.h>
main()
{
```

```
    int array[100], n, c, d, position, swap;
    printf("Enter number of elements\n");
    scanf("%d", &n);
    printf("Enter %d integers\n", n);
    for ( c = 0 ; c < n ; c++ ) {
      scanf("%d", &array[c]);
  }
    for ( c = 0 ; c < ( n - 1 ) ; c++ ) {
      position = c;
      for ( d = c + 1 ; d < n ; d++ ) {
        if ( array[position] > array[d] )
          position = d;
      }
    if ( position != c ) {
        swap = array[c];
        array[c] = array[position];
        array[position] = swap;
      }
   }
   printf("Sorted list in ascending order:\n");
  for ( c = 0 ; c < n ; c++ )
    printf("%d\n", array[c]);
  return 0;
}
```

Output 13.2

```
1    2    3    4    5    6    7    8    9    10
```

Example 13.3

Printing Tri-graphs On Console

```
#include <stdio.h>
int main(void) {
        printf ("\n ??= Hello C ??= \n");
        return 0;
}
```

Output 13.3

Compile:

gcc -trigraphs file_name.c

command to enable trigraphs without this option warning generates and trigraphs ignored by gcc compiler

Run:

./a.out //execute programe

Output:— # Hello C #

Example 13.4

Create Logger file for client application.

```
#include<stdio.h>
#include<string.h>
void writeMessageToLoggerFile(char debugMessage[20]) {
        FILE *filePtr;
        filePtr = fopen("HomeAutomationLogger.log", "w");
        if (filePtr == NULL) {
        printf("Error in operning file HomeAutomationLogger.log
        \n");
        }
fprintf(filePtr,"FileName: %s \nFunctionName: %s \nLine No: %d : Called From
: %s\n“,__FILE__,__func__,__LINE__, debugMessage);
```

```
        fclose(filePtr);
}
int main() {
        char message[20];
        writeMessageToLoggerFile(strcpy(message,__func__));
        return 0;
}
```

Output 13.4

```
FileName: HomeAutomationLogger.cpp
FunctionName: writeMessageToLoggerFile
Line No: 10 : Called From : main
```

Example 13.5

Program to load functions before start and end of execution

```
#include <stdio.h>
void CallFunctionOnStart() __attribute__((constructor));
void CallFunctionOnEnd() __attribute__((destructor));
void CallFunctionOnStart() {
        printf("Function Name: %s Called At Start\n”,__func__);
        printf("Code To Load Shared Library\n");
}
void CallFunctionOnEnd() {
        printf("Function Name: %s Called At Exit\n”,__func__);
        printf("Code To UnLoad Shared Library\n");
}
int main()  {
printf("Functiona Name: %s\nLine No: %d\n",__func__,__LINE__);
        return 0;
}
```

Output 13.5

Function Name: CallFunctionOnStart Called At Start

Code To Load Shared Library

Function Name: main

Line No: 25

Function Name: CallFunctionOnEnd Called At Exit

Code To UnLoad Shared Library

Example: 13.6

Dynamic Memory Allocation using malloc and creating linked-list for memory allocation

```
struct Memory {
        void *v_ptrContent;
        struct Memory *nextMemoryBlock;
        // self referencing pointer to struct member points to next // address
        }
int main() {
        struct Memory *memBlock1 = (struct Memory *)
        malloc((sizeof(struct Memory )));
        struct Memory *memBlock2 = (struct Memory *)
        malloc((sizeof(struct Memory )));
        struct Memory *memBlock3 = (struct Memory *)
        malloc((sizeof(struct Memory )));
 memBlock1->nextMemoryBlock = memBlock2;
 memBlock2->nextMemoryBlock = memBlock3;
 memBlock3->nextMemoryBlock = NULL;
                //end block is pointing to NULL
 int a1 = 100;     //following info is stored at particular memory DMA
        technique
 memBlock1->v_ptrContent = malloc(sizeof(int));
```

```
memBlock1->v_ptrContent = &a1; // Info stored in void pointer
memBlock2->v_ptrContent = malloc(sizeof(int));
memBlock2->v_ptrContent = memBlock1->v_ptrContent;
memBlock3->v_ptrContent = malloc(sizeof(int));
memBlock3->v_ptrContent = memBlock2->v_ptrContent;
// following while loop displays v-ptrContent on console
// memory block is pointing to some address and info, content // is shown on console
while(memBlock1) {
printf("Node = %d\n",*(int *)memBlock1->v_ptrContent);
memBlock1 = memBlock1->nextMemoryBlock;
}
```

Output 13.6

Node 1 = 100

Node 2 = 100

Node 3 = 100

Example 13.7

Write a code snippet to perform matrix addition and multiplication. Use functions to pass matrix variable of type array.

```
#include <stdio.h>
void readMatrixElements(int matrix[3][3]) {
printf("Enter Matrix Element of Size 3 x 3 \n");
for(int index1 = 0;index1 < 3;index1++) {
        for(int index2 = 0;index2 < 3;index2++) {
                scanf("%d",&matrix[index1][index2]);
                }
        }
}
```

```
void displayMatrix(const int matrix[3][3]) {
printf("Matrix Element of Size 3 x 3 :\n");
for(int index1 = 0;index1 < 3;index1++) {
        for(int index2 = 0;index2 < 3;index2++) {
                printf("%d ",matrix[index1][index2]);
                }
                printf("\n");
        }
}
void addEigenVectors(int vector1[3][3],int vector2[3][3]) {
        printf("Addition Of Vectors\n");
        for(int index1 =0;index1<3;index1++) {
                for(int index2 =0;index2<3;index2++) {
                vector1[index1][index2] = vector1[index1][index2]
                                        +
            vector2[index1][index2];
                                        }
                                }
                }
void multiplyMatrix(int vector1[3][3], int vector2[3][3], int
                                        resultantVector[3][3]) {
        for(int rowIndex = 0;rowIndex<3;rowIndex++) {
                for(int colIndex = 0;colIndex < 3;colIndex++) {
                resultantVector[rowIndex][colIndex] = 0;
                }
        }
printf("Multiplication Of Added Vector and Vector Matrix 2 \n");
        for(int rowIndex = 0;rowIndex<3;rowIndex++) {
```

```
                for(int colIndex =0;colIndex<3;colIndex++) {
                for(int colIndexIn = 0;colIndexIn<3;colIndexIn++) {
                resultantVector[rowIndex][colIndex] += \
        (vector1[rowIndex][colIndexIn] * vector2[colIndexIn]
                                                    [colIndex]);
                            }
                    }
        }
}
int main() {
        int matrixOfEigenVector1[3][3]={0};
        int matrixOfEigenVector2[3][3]={0};
        int resultantVectorMatrix[3][3] = {0};
        readMatrixElements(matrixOfEigenVector1);
        readMatrixElements(matrixOfEigenVector2);
        //displayed Input Matrix
        displayMatrix(matrixOfEigenVector1);
        displayMatrix(matrixOfEigenVector2);

        //Added Two Matrices and Displayed Matrix Added
        addEigenVectors(matrixOfEigenVector1,matrixOfEigenVector2);
        displayMatrix(matrixOfEigenVector1);

        //Matrix Multiplication Of Two matrices of Eigen vectors values

multiplyMatrix(matrixOfEigenVector1,matrixOfEigenVector2,resultantVector
Matrix);

        displayMatrix(resultantVectorMatrix);
```

```
        return 0;
}
```

Output 13.7

```
Matrix Element of Size 3 x 3 :
1 1 1
1 1 1
1 1 1
Matrix Element of Size 3 x 3 :
2 2 2
2 2 2
2 2 2
Addition Of Vectors
Matrix Element of Size 3 x 3 :
3 3 3
3 3 3
3 3 3
Multiplication Of Added Vector and Vector Matrix 2
Matrix Element of Size 3 x 3 :
18 18 18
18 18 18
18 18 18
```

Example 13.8

Compare Product Id using String C API.

```
#include <stdio.h>
#include <string.h>
int main() {
const char *productId1 = "123456789";
```

```
const char *productId2 = "123456789";
if (strcmp(productId1,productId2) == 0)
printf("ProductIDs %s and %s are equal\n",productId1,productId2);
else
printf("ProductIDs %s and %s are not euqal \n", productId1, productId2);
const char *productId3 = "12345";
if (strcmp(productId2,productId3) == 0)
printf("ProductIDs %s and %s are euqal \n ", productId2, productId3);
else
printf("ProductIDs %s and %s are not equal \n",productId2, productId3);
return 0;
}
```

Output 13.8

```
ProductIDs 123456789 and 123456789 are euqal
ProductIDs 123456789 and 12345 are not euqal
```

Topic Covered in Part II

C++ Language Programming

Chapter 14. Introduction to C++

14.1 Introduction

In C programming language as a programmer you will not find much difficulties in coding, but as you progress and bring projects for development phase, facilities or I will say inbuilt tools available which perform ease of development C++ is much more superior than C language. But as author many great designs of development are performed using C programming language. So never under estimate C programming since C++ is a superior set of C language only. C++ support all features of C language along with its own features making a well organized programming language for development of todays real world projects.

Issues faced by C language are data is openly move around system organization. So binding of data is not happened effectively in C as compared to C++. In C all members are public so there is no access restriction provided by language. C++ have access restriction feature that restrict open movement of information within organization of system. It allows better control and more security to information. Information is private by default inside C++.

C is called procedural language as one procedure calls another procedure and another so on. It is complete nesting of procedure calls to one other. Procedure is normally called function in C that we seen in previous discussion of this book. I consider you are well verse with C syntax. Now onwards our aim is to look at the C++ aspect of learning.

C++ is called object oriented language as one object calls many procedures belongs to that object and keep passing information to another object of same or different type with the help of procedural parameters. In such a case information means variables are contained in objects and not moving openly around system organization but communicated with the help of object oriented procedure calls. This way of programming gives lots of ease of programming and ways to handle information in system memory on execution of application. This new way of programming is called OOPs methodology i.e. Object Oriented Programming in C++. C++ is extension of C. C++ allows logical partition of information into object memory as variable memory set which is unique to individual object created and a procedure memory common to all variables of individual object set belongs to information set. In OOPs information is shared with the help of functions through respective call by objects.

In OOPs, classes are considered as blueprint of objects and objects are considered as instance of class. Now to look at this definition in little different angle, we considered class as "PRODUCT WITH COMPONENT" and its behavior is defined by its "FEATURES". So at point we can say that a class with its attribute and behavior considered as a "PRODUCT WITH COMPONENTS AND ITS FEATURES". By Example, a CAR is product with its components and its behavior is modeled by CARs features.

Now as we consider product as a class made of different components, a components possibly another class, made of components. For example, to explain this scenario consider a home automation system in customer needs to interact with digital switch board, here switch board is final product so a class with its components and features. Now to operate switch board we need buttons, so here "Pushbutton" is another class made of its components and its own features that make up final product called product class. We can say that component can be look like a well define class. Product features and component features make up final PRODUCT and its features together.

14.2 Features Introduce In C++

1. Classes
2. Objects
3. Encapsulation
4. Abstraction
5. Polymorphism
6. Inheritance
7. Static and Dynamic Binding to procedural calls

14.2.1 Classes

In C++ ' class ' keyword is used to create class of particular family. To explain this scenario consider a home automation system in customer needs to interact with digital switch board. In this case developer creates a class called SwitchBoard and includes all the functionality required to create a board. Then with the help of class keyword he defines class including all members and functions required to define or operate switch board. Once this is made the next step is to create as many switch board objects required for particularly home automation system.

e.g. class SwitchBoard { … };

14.2.2 Objects

In section classes we define class called SwitchBoard. Now we have to create a variable of type SwitchBoard. Such a member or variable is called object of class called SwitchBoard. Object is created by following class name followed by variable name.

e.g. SwitchBoard SB1,SB2;

So here SB1 and SB2 are objects of user-defined type i.e. not built-in type. These are used to access members of SwitchBoard class.

14.2.3 Encapsulation

In encapsulation technique actually it is a methodology where required member variables and functions are defined inside class. In this its conventional that members are written into private section and functions are written into public section of class. So once class is defined hold both together as a single entity. In this way entry to members is only made available via public section of a class. Other way is not possible. Encapsulation is a methodology to hold class members and functions together inside class defined is called encapsulation. In this information remains hidden to outside world of class define. Also known as data hiding or information hiding or restricting access to information or data.

14.2.4 Abstraction

Abstraction is a process of defining all parameters required for particular class say SwitchBoard. Class holds member variables and procedural names inside class body written. Members hold information and functions hold operations performed on information. Abstraction is a process of defining member variables and functions that are sufficient to complete the requirements of class. Classes use methodology of abstraction are called abstract(A) data(D) type(T) i.e. (ADT).

e.g.

```
class SwitchBoard {
private:
        Button mFan1;
        Button mFan2;
```

```
        Button mTubeLight;
public:
        void onFanOneButton() { … }
        void onFanTwoButton() { … }
        void onTubeLightButton() { … }
};
```

14.2.5 Polymorphism

This a technique used mainly in dynamic binding. In this technique same function name or operator inbuilt behaviour is assign another task of same role. They are one is 'function' overloading and another is 'operator' overloading. In function overloading function name is kept constant and depending on information pass call to respective function is made either by static or dynamic binding. In operator overloading case built-in operators are used to perform operation on user-defined type like on two object addition or string objects addition with the help of '+' plus operator in C++. In both cases polymorphic form must be defined explicitly by programmer or developer to enjoy polymorphism. Poly means many and morphism means forms so single name with multiple functionality is called polymorphism in C++.

14.2.6 Inheritance

This is a technique used to use existing feature of predefined class and extending features of user defined class is called inheritance. In this mechanism features are added to predefined class by defining new class and inheriting old class.

This is hierarchical extension by introducing new class to serve purpose and to follow single responsibility principle. In inheritance more general class seats at the top of hierarchical classification and single responsible class seats at the bottom of inheritance hierarchy.

14.2.7 Static and Dynamic Binding to procedural calls

- **Static Binding**

It is a technique used to link static information to procedure. To explain this scenario consider a home automation system in customer needs to interact with digital switch board and each option on switch board to its name by specifying string so that it will appear on switch board for its smooth operation. This kind of binding is called static binding where information is known to objects at compile time and shown on UI at run time by application.

- **Dynamic Binding**

It is a technique used to link dynamic information to procedure at run time. To explain this scenario considers a home automation system in customer needs to interact with digital switch board button. Now in digital switch board customer need to add lamp button without opening switch board at run time of application since provision is already provided. So application is already in running mode and customer is able to create button to operate newly added lamp in home automation system. In this scenario information available is loaded at runtime without disturbing existing functionality of automation system. This kind of binding is called dynamic binding where information is known is loaded in objects at run-time and shown on UI at run-time by application without affecting existing functionality.

14.3 Summary

- This chapter is a introduction to C++ language. New features are added to C language discuss earlier.
- Features added to C are classes, objects, abstraction and encapsulation, Inheritance and polymorphism.
- So what are classes and its objects? It is a blueprint of objects and objects are instance of a class.
- Encapsulation and abstraction are nothing but how data move around system app and its visibility to different section of a class and app. Encapsulation is binding information to its members with limited or required exposure is call data hiding. Information is not openly passes from one another. They are bound to objects for communication.
- Inheritance is feature added to C to extend features of structure. Structures are public in C and there is no way we can extend information from one another structures. This kind of way of programming by extending features of one class by another class is called Inheritance in C++.
- Polymorphism is a response to same things but different way. Basically poly means multiple and morphism means different behavior. Polymorphism is a response to same instance by calling different overloaded and virtual methods.

- Static and Dynamic bindings are refer to linkage of code to its library at compile time (static) and or at run time (dynamically). Linkage of source code to its executable is referred as binding in C++.

14.4 Hausaufgaben

- Read Google about it.
- Read Google about Classes and Objects
- Read Abstraction and Encapsulation
- Read about Inheritance and Polymorphism

Chapter 15.
Let's Begin C++

In this we come across new way of reading I/O different than conventional C way. This chapter introduce new keywords introduce by C++ in addition to existing C keyword set. C++ support all the keywords of C but reverse is not true.

15.1 Printing and Reading Data

Printing and reading data on console in C++ is quite easy. C++ provides two operators are called insertion (<<) operator and extraction (>>) operator respectively. They are used with 'cout' and 'cin'. To print information on console information must be inserted into output stream. The operator helps in performing task is called insertion (<<) operator. Similarly to extract information from input stream and assigns to variable programmer needs extraction (>>) operator. With '<<' and '>>' multiple info allowed to print and read from console. Suppose programmer wants to inform customer on console based application that "Your Total Bill Amount Is 200 INR". So he does like this as follows in C++ language,

```
int mAmountToBePaid = 0;
mAmountToBePaid         = 200;
cout<<"Your Total Bill Amount Is "<< lAmountToBePaid <<" INR \n";
        //...\n for newline
```

Similarly we can print multiple text as well as variables following above pattern.

```
cout<<"City Name"<<cityname<<"Building Name" << building-
name<<"\n";
```

In the same way programmer wants to read customer product price from console based application by using >> insertion operator along with 'cin'. Suppose customer goes to shopping mall and purchase three products. Now he comes to payment console then how payment console application reads three products as below,

```
float lProduct1 = 0;
float lProduct2 = 0;
```

```
float lProduct2 = 0;
cout<<"Enter Product Price "<<" \n";
cin>>lProduct1>>lProduct2>>lProduct3;
```

Now after reading product price 30 40 60 total bill is generated and receipt is dispatch to the customer. Now a days UI is available along with barcode reading machine, reads product price and generates bill. Information is extracted from barcode reader and process by application. Header file used to perform IO is iostream.h along with it programmer must specify following statement "using namespace std;". With the help of these two programmer is capable to write standard IO operation program.

15.2 Keywords In C++

C++ is a superset of C therefore support all the keyword available in C along with additional keywords specified below.

1. delete	2. Catch	3. try	4.class
5.friend	6. inline	7. private	8. public
9.protected	10. new	11. virtual	12. this
13. throw	14. template	15. asm	16. bool
17. true	18. false	19. mutable	20. static_cast
21. dynamic_cast	22. reinterpret_cast	23.const_cast	24. Typeid
25. namespace	26. using	27. wchar_t	28. typename
29. explicit	30. operator	31. void pointer (void *)	
32. export	33. endl		

15.2.1 Keywords Explained In C++

Operator/Keyword	Explanation
delete	This keyword is used to delete memory allocation by new operator
catch	This keyword is used to acquire expression thrown by throw statement inside try block
try	this keyword is used to throw unhanded conditions from this block
throw	throws condition that is not handled by application

class	this keyword is used to create/group certain features together assignee unit with visibility of each variables
friend	This keyword is used to access common private information between two or more class by making friend of each other class
inline	this keyword is used to have expansion like macro calls of single line statement inside functions
private	This keyword restrict access to particular info specified under private keyword
public	This keyword restrict access to particular info specified under public keyword. Usually public means full access similar to structures in C.
protected	This keyword is used to access limited visibility to code. Used mostly in case of inheritance.
new	This keyword is used to allocates memory on heap
virtual	This keyword is used to perform dynamic polymorphism during Inheritance.
this	This keyword is used to represent current invoking object on function calls.
template	This keyword is used to perform generic programming with help of compiler to specify code at compile time.
asm	This keyword is used to define assembly in C++.
bool	This keyword is used to define boolean type in code.
true	This keyword is used to indicates status of bool type variable as true value.
false	This keyword is used to indicates status of bool type variable as false value.
mutable	This keyword is used to remove constant ness of variable.
static_cast	This keyword is used to convert or type cast from one type to another type of primitive type variables. Ex. float amtToPay = 1.5; int netAmtToPay = static_cast<int>(amtToPay); O/P = netAmtToPay = 1;
dynamic_cast	This keyword is used to convert or type cast from one type to another type of user-define type variables say object of classes. Ex. Convert Derived Class to its Base Class baseClassObj = dynamic_cast<Base*>(derivedClassObj)

reinterpret_cast	This keyword is used to convert or type cast from one type to another type of primitive type variables to pointer type and vice-versa.
const_cast	This keyword is used to override constant-ness or volatileness.
typeid	This keyword is used to extract type info of a primitive and user-defined type object in type_info datatype. It requires <typeinfo> header file.
namespace	This keyword is used to resolve naming convention when mismatch happen for user specified variables or built0in type variables
using	This keyword is used to apply namespace for particular type when conflict occurs.
wchar_t	This keyword is used to specify character of 2byte long as usually char is one byte long.
typename	This keyword is used to define type name of variables and not its type.
explicit	This keyword is used to prevent copy initialisation and implicit conversion. Used along with constructor of a class.
operator	This keyword is used to define user-specific operators without changing original meaning of operator
void pointer	This datatype is used to represent generic type that can be converted to specific and required type.
export	This keyword is used to export libraries in projects from one module to another by specifying export keyword
endl	This keyword is used to feed a complete line at the output of previous line.

15.3 Reference Variable

In C references to base variable are specified with the help of pointers and later dereferencing pointer variable to see change in original information. In this process pointer variable occupies additional memory location. To remedies to above situation C++ specifies another approach to mitigate additional memory occupancy issue with reference variable (&). With reference variable same memory location is used rather assigning additional memory to reference variable and information is modified in memory. To explain this scenario consider a home automation system in customer needs to interact with digital switch board and with single switch turn off all electrical equipment in home automation system. So we assume that customer is going outstation for few days. In this case developer make switch to zero so automatically it makes switch off all electric equipments connected to home automation system rather switching off individual equipments by customer. In this safety and safe shutting of home automation makes better performed and saves electrical devices from abrupt electrical interference. This kind of programming is used mostly in embedded devices to ensure closing protocol. Developer or programmer cannot assigns constant values to reference variables. Modifying information by reference technique is called "call by reference". Reference variable should be initializing at the time of its declaration shown in below syntax.

Syntax:

```
data-type  variableName = initialValue;

data-type & referenceVariableName = variableName;
```

Example:

```
int mProductId   = 10001;

int & mReferenceProductId = mProductId;

mReferenceProductId = 10003;
```

So in above example mReferenceProductId and mProductId both values changes to 10003 since modifies through reference variable technique. In above method original information in mProductId lost and new information assign is stored in both variables.

So now, mReferenceProductId = 10003;

mProductId = 10003;

15.4 Newly Introduce Operators In C++

In C++ many new features are added over conventional methodology of C programming to facilitates and reduce programming as well as development and redevelopment overhead of coding efforts. In previous section we learn about IO operators. In this we see more newly introduce operators of C++ language.

Operator	Operator Fuctionality
delete	Releases memory allocated through new operator on system heap
new	Allocates sufficient memory on heap of size data members included in objects and returns initial address on allocation
: :	Operator is called scope resolution operator, resolves scope of local variable in context to immediate global variable.
: :*	Pointer to member of a class declarator. Operator is used to declared pointer to member of a class
.*	Pointer to member operator. Operator is used to access member variables declared in class using object and a pointer to member
—>*	Pointer to member operator. Operator is used to access member variables declared using pointer to object and a pointer to member

- Advantages using new and delete operator over C malloc() and calloc() and free()as below

8. new operator calculates the size of memory required for memory allocation on heap so that programmer or developer need not use sizeof operator explicitly.
9. On allocation of memory on head returns appropriate datatype so no need of typecast memory pointer. C++ is very strict about specifying type. If datatype miss-match is happened compiler generates error or sometimes warning message.
10. In C++ we have new feature called operator overloading applicable to new and delete operator same way as with other overloadable operators. In C++ certain operators are restricted to use operator overloading feature. Simply you can not overload as this feature is not available to them.
11. new operator automatically resize its memory allocation on heap on demand by object at run-time. In case of malloc resize of memory is made with calloc function call. You can not use malloc for resize of memory in C.

15.5 Summary

- In this chapter we learn about different keywords are introducing in C++ and its explanation.
- There are total 32 keywords are introduce in C++ apart from 11 keywords are reserved and only available to compiler use.

- Operator "new, delete, *:: and -->*" are not allow for overloading or used to change fundamental meaning of rules.
- To access memory C++ uses pointer type called as variable references. We cannot assign one reference to another.
- Later you will learn advantages and disadvantages of new and delete over malloc() and free() functions.

15.6 HousaufGaben

1. Read More about References variables in C++.
2. Read Operators in C++.
3. Read about heterogeneous Read and Write in C++.
4. See new and malloc examples along with delete and realloc and calloc.

NOTES

Chapter 16.
Functions Feature in C++

In programming world particular block of code needs to be reuse again and again. Modular approach and classifying and dividing functionality into sections or by organizing programming logic have great importance and impact on project cost and development time. To explain this scenario considers a home automation system in customer needs to interact with digital switch called switch button or key to operate switch board. Now to there are five LEDs to be operated. In this switch functionality is same across multiple switches. So the job of developer is to have common module or function name that operates switch. Such a common module is written by programmer or developer is called modular programming and module is called functions. If such a function grows by number of lines then sub divided into sub-modules. These modules then called multiple times in program reduces effort by developer in coding. In functions many times required to define functionality by name of module. To explain this scenario considers a home automation system in multiple images to put on UI. In this developer gives "putImageOnUI" with different arguments to for different images with multiple definitions by keeping same module name is called module overloading i.e. function overloading in C++. This feature is not available in C programming. Another is that same function to be called in different modules by initiating with different modules is called visual functions in C++ by implementing its interfaces in calling module.

Syntax:

```
return-type function-name ( data-type arg1,  data-type arg2,
                    ...) {
        return info;
}
```

Example:

```
SWITCH ledSwitchOn(SWITCH LED_ON) {
        ...
        return SWITCH_ON_LED;
```

}

In functions you can always have default arguments to function such as NULL argument to functions receive pointer type object can be overloaded by argument passed. original argument i.e. default argument is then ignored by function on reception otherwise not.

16.1 Types of Function

With above discussion functions are classified into following categories

1. Non-Parameterized Functions
2. Parameterized Functions
3. Function With Default Arguments
4. Function with Return type
5. Overloaded Functions
6. Inline Functions
7. Friend Functions
8. Virtual Functions

- Non-Parameterized Functions

In this category parameter list or argument-list is empty. Such a function or module does not receive any information in its argument list neither NULL nor any type. Such a argument list is specifies void type indicating no argument. Such a function is called "non-parameterized" function.

syntax:

```
return-type Function-name ( void ) {
        return info;
}
```

Example1:

```
bool switchOnLED ( void ) {
        return bLEDOn;
}
```

Example2:

```
bool switchOnLED ( ) {
        return bLEDOn;
}
```

- Parameterized Functions, Function With Default Arguments And Function with Return type

These types of function at least have single parameter as an argument is called parameterized function. These parameterized functions have default argument then it's called default parameterized function or function with default argument.

Syntax:

```
return-type Function-name ( arg1, arg2, …) {
        return info;
}
```

Example1:

It indicates LEDs on switch board are either made on or off by passing parameter.

```
bool switchOnLED ( const bool bLED ) {
        return bLEDOn;
}
```

Example2:

It indicates LEDs on switch board are off by default.

```
bool switchOnLED ( bool bLEDOn = false ) {
        return bLEDOn;
}
```

- Overloaded Functions

In this same function name is used with different types of arguments such as char, int, float etc. Use of arguments shouldn't leads to integral promotion of built-in type. If this happened then compiler gives error that overloading is not possible with that particular type. e.g. float to double. Function overloading is achieved by changing argument list and type of argument list in parameter specification of module or function.

Syntax:

```
return-type Function-name ( arg1, arg2, ...)          {
        return info;    }
```

Examples:

```
bool putImageOnUI ( iDesktop ) {
return true;
}
bool putImageOnUI ( iLaptop ) {
return true;
}
bool putImageOnUI ( iMobile, iPod ) {
return true;
}
bool putImageOnUI ( iSmartTV ) {
return true;
}
```

- Inline Functions

Inline functions are used when functions are small in size by having few lines then such a function is tag with "inline" keyword. The purpose of inline function is to have less execution time and reusability and modular approach to design. Less execution time is achieve through macro definition of function. In macro definitions actual function call is replaced by MACRO statement. In case of call, control is transferred to its definition for execution but i case of MACRO call is replaced by actual code and then it executed. Inline functions are useful in case of less lines inside function body along with return.

If the function contains static variables, goto , loop, switch, recursive call then function cannot be treated as inline function but as only function call. This function call will not be replace by Macro calls and not have privilege of execution of statements like without stacking function call in code execution.

Syntax:

```
inline return-type function-name(arg1, arg2, ..) {
        return (statement to be executed in line);
}
```

Example:

```
inline int putProductOnUI (int num1, int num2) {
        return (num1 * num2);
}
```

- Friend Functions

These functions are used to have common access of information between two classes where access of information is restricted to public flow of info. These restrictions are achieved with the help of abstraction and encapsulations methodology. Friend function is declared with "friend" keyword as a global function which have access to restricted info become member of two or more than this classes. We will discuss more when we see classes and its use.

- Virtual Functions

Virtual functions are use to achieve run-time polymorphism or late or dynamic binding. Dynamic bindings are achieved with virtual table concept. We will discuss these functions in inheritance technique of reusing code.

16.2 Calling C function in C++

In development of application, functionality is not directly available in single platform. For example I am developing home automation system using ARM controller. Now to write functionality i need various pre-built libraries to ease/simplify my work of coding. Many times hardware core are develop by developer own proprietary so without permission we cannot use to develop project. Or otherwise customer of this intellectual-property agreed on license agreement like open source agreement. Otherwise open source libraries need to be use by agreed upon open source license agreement. You need to publish your project code in which open source libraries are used. These are called "intellectual property" of devices in the form of hardware library cores.

```
// CFunctionPrototypeHeaderFile.h
#ifdef __cplusplus
extern "C" {
```

```
#endif
//all your c functions prototype required to invoke in cpp
void C_function1( int );
void C_function2( double );
void C_functionN( char *);
#ifdef __cplusplus
}
#endif
```

16.3 Summary

- In this chapter, we learn about creating functions and its use. Why functions are important in OOPs kind of programming languages.
- It is good approach to have modular program that handles particular module.
- In modular programming, easy to detect errors and correct it.
- So based on functions parameter and return type are classified into non-parameterized and parameterized functions.
- Also depends on arguments are fixed or variable are classified as default functions.
- Also by variation of arguments and their type classified as overloaded function and so on as explain above.

16.4 Housaufgaben

1. Write short note on functions. Classify functions based on type, name, parameter and its arguments.
2. Create a class called MyHomeAutomationLoginPageUI and define functions to read credential such as myHomeAutomatiionLoginName, myHomeAutomatiionLoginId, myHomeAutomatiionLoginPassword.
3. Verify its accountability and grant operation to perform on Home Automation system.
4. Add more features as per your convenience and understanding.

Chapter 17.
Classes And Its Features

In classes and its features are concern about the concept called abstraction and encapsulation and polymorphism. The classes we discuss are not about school or college terminology I know you are aware so just kidding. The classes is a organization of storage of computer like device memory into different segments like private, public and protected parts by using regular memory area. In classes private are accessible only through public section and not by another path in computer memory lines. So to have access of private section of class developer must communicates becoming member of public section inside class. Acquiring communication must acquired public section and then private in that manner. By looking software side of class, it is a keyword that declares a block of software or programme area containing variables, member functions together as a single block. Classes have certain rules and regulations for access and specify info inside it. Classes represents not only single entity but can be extended too. Classes are extension of C structures where only public members are present.

17.1 Classes In C++

Class is program block in programming language C++ used to abstract and encapsulate information and to represent the way to access it by classifying it as private and public sections. This way developer creates class type variable get access to class information. The variable of class type in program memory is called object of class. Some books called it as a run-time entity in execution indicates same.

Syntax:

```
class className {
        private:
                data-type variableName1;
                data-type variableName2;
                ...
        public:
```

```
                    data-type variableName;
                    data-type variableName;
                    function-name1;
                    ...
        };
```

Example:

```
class switchBoard {
        Button mSWBButton1;
        Button mSWBButton2;
        LED mLEDLight1;
        LED mLEDLight2;
        Regulator       mRegulatorSW;
        int     mMaxRegulatorSpeed;
public:
        void createButton() {
        ...     }
        void ledLight() {
        ...     }
        void createRegulator() {
        ...     }
        int getMaxRegulatorSpeed() {
        ...
        return mMaxRegulatorSpeed;
        }
        void onLEDLight ( LED lLEDNumber);
//written outside class see below
};
```

In above example only public sections are shown. If keyword is not specified then by default section is private otherwise specified section.

17.2 Object In C++

Now we seen that how class is written and information is recorded inside class. After record of information its obvious that it needs to be access and used by client for business purpose. Some mechanism is required to access class info. To facilitates such a access entity is define called "object" of a class. With the help of object only public members are accessed and not private info. Private info is access through public members. Hiding info from direct access from objects of same class is called data hiding.

Syntax:

```
class-name object-name;

object-name.function-name(arg1, arg2, ...);
// public section function-name

object.variable-name;
// public section variable-name
```

With the help of dot (.) operator functions and variables are accessible belongs to public section of class.

Example:

```
switchBoard switchBoardSwitch;

int maxRegulatorSpeed =
swicthBoardSwitch.getMaxRegulatorSpeed();

cout<<"Switch Board Regulator Maximum Speed = "<<
maxRegulatorSpeed <<endl;

swicthBoardSwitch.mLEDLight1;

// If LEDLight1 is public section variable
```

17.3 Defining Member Function In C++

There are two ways to write member function belongs to a particular class. One is inside class and another is outside class body by writing function prototype inside class and function body outside class. First way is we seen in previous section. In second case syntax is written below,

Syntax:

```
        return-type class-name : : funation-name ( arg1, arg2, …)    access-
specifier
        {
                …
                body
                return (Info / Variable / Object);
        }
```

One member function are calling another member function belongs to same class without help of object of class. This is called nesting of member functions of a class. Even privately written member functions are nested inside public member functions. To define scope outside class context programmer must use scope resolution (: :) operator.

Example:

```
        LED switchBoard : : onLEDLight ( LED lLEDNumber) {
                …
                body
                return lLEDNumber; }
```

17.4 Allocating Memory Block To Class Type

In programming world, to avail information access within out outside programme scope needs to be allocated in either stack or in heap memory section. Since stack is limited heap also limited but huge in size for enough allocation which is permanent during lifecycle of application. In case of objects there are two requirements of allocating memory one on stack and heap. Inside class we can specify both variables and functions unlike structure only variables and not functions. It is requirement of having memory allocation for both statements. Whenever object is instantiated of a class in memory each copy of variable are created and common for function for each copy of objects of same class. Functions have common memory and variables have individual copy separately. Function memory is shared between between calls but not variables memory.

Illustration of allocating memory block to class type is made available below,

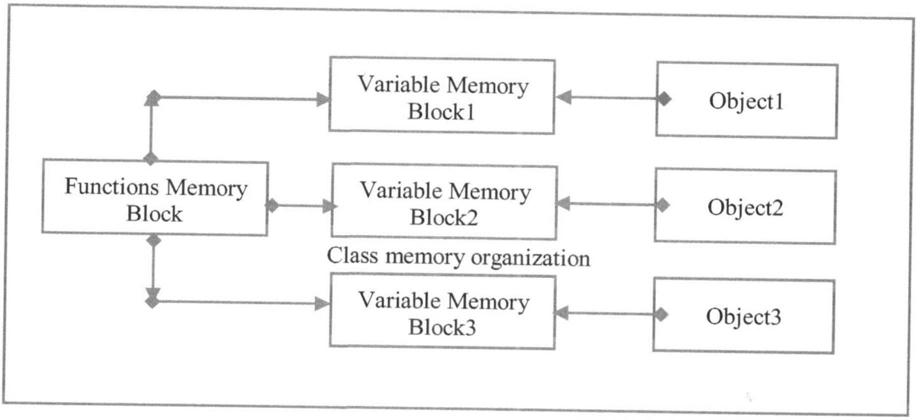

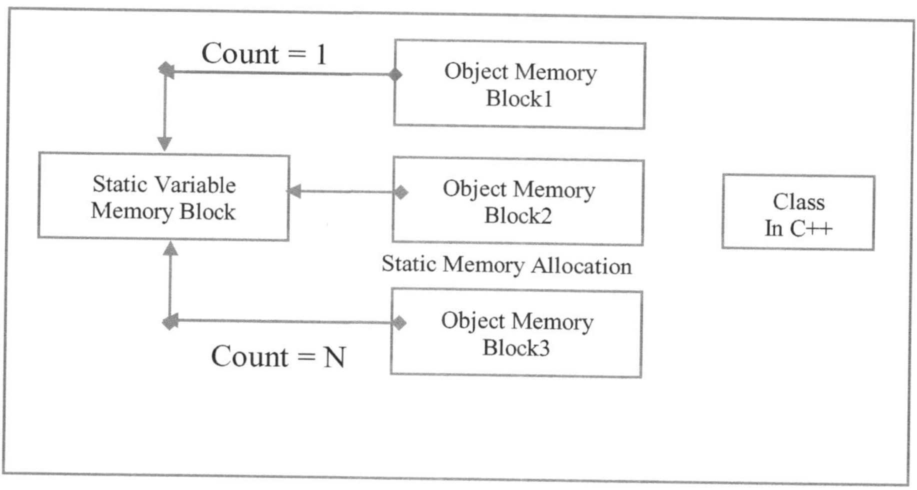

17.5 Static Variable Inside Class

Before explanation just shown figure for self-explanatory concept.

As said by static keyword single copy is shared between multiple calls. In the same way static member variable copy is shared between multiple copies of object of same class. As above figure completely explains static variable life scenario. Static variables are initialises to zero if no initialisation is provided by programmer.

Syntax:

```
static data-type variableName; // declaration of static
                    variable inside class
```

```
data-type class-name :: variable-name; // initialisation of
                              static variable to zero
```

Example:

// Incrementing static-variable by increment operator inside incrementSerialNo() function call.

```
static int mSerialNo;

int SerialRecord : : mSerialNo;

object-name1.incrementSerialNo();

object-name2.incrementSerialNo();

object-name3.incrementSerialNo();
```

when you print mSerialNo on console indicates three value with three different objects of same class and not different class objects. Each object have separate copy of variables in memory but not static variables. To explain this scenario consider the example of databases used to maintain customer transactions in computer will me maintained by creating static variable;

17.6 Static Function Inside Class

In static function access only static variables of same class. These functions are not allow to access non-static types inside function of same class. Static functions are class using class name of the same class and using scope resolution operator (: :). To explain this scenario consider a example of showing particular record number track with static variable. Now each counted record to be shown on UI for customer reference. In that case static functions are used rather than non-static function calls.

Syntax:

```
call to static function made as below,

class-name : : function-name ( arg1, arg2, …);
```

Example:

```
switchBoard : : showUI();
```

17.7 Friend Class

We can make all the members of one class accessible by another class by making friend of that class. These are development requirements of application in C++.

Many times in programming field and in implementing single responsibility principle and specifying access to private data members friend class is required for ease of development. A class can be friend of another class by making friend of that class.

Syntax:

```
friend class class-name;
```

Example:

```
friend class switchBoard;
```

17.8 Forward Specification

In C++ one class needs objects of another class to call its members inside another. In such a case including its header creates compilation errors of each other class. To mitigate issue C++ suggest to have forward specification of class in respective header file wherever needed. This kind of relationship is called "has a" relationship in which class contains object of another class inside it. And when class is inherited with some another class is class "is a" relationship. So said like class is a inherited from another class.

Syntax:

```
class-name objectName; //Forward specification of class
```

Example:

```
class LEDLights; // forward declaration
// forward specification with respective of class Lights
class Lights {
        LEDLights obj;
        // class Lights uses class LEDLights object inside it.
        // needs forward specification of class LEDLights.
};
class LEDLights {
// class LEDLights not uses class Lights object inside it.
};
```

17.9 Function Pointers In C++

Function pointers in C and C++ are called call-back functions. In this approach call to function is made by strictly calling from address in library and not having stack entry of calling functions. So call is made from outside entry by using call-back function.

Syntax:

Step1: create static or dynamic class object.

className objectName;

OR

className *objectName;

Step2: Create function pointer belongs to particular class by using class name as below

return-type (*classname::function-pointer-variable)
(arg1,arg2,...) =
&classname::functionname-without-parameter-list;

Step3: Call to function through function pointer variable

(objectName.*function-pointer-variable)

(arg1, arg2, ...);

OR

(objectName->*function-pointer-variable)

(arg1, arg2, ...);

Example:

```
#include<iostream>
using namespace std;
class switchBoard {
public:
    void getMaxRegulatorSpeed() {
    cout<<"CallBackWithPointerToMember\n";
    }
```

```
};
int main() {
        switchBoard *sb;            //method1
        void (switchBoard :: *sb_ptr)(void) = &
        switchBoard::getMaxRegulatorSpeed;
        ( sb->*sb_ptr )();// call to function by call-back methods
        switchBoard swb; //method2
        void (switchBoard :: *swb_ptr)(void) = &
        switchBoard::getMaxRegulatorSpeed;
        ( swb.*swb_ptr )();
        // call to function by call-back methods
}
```

17.10 Summary

- In this chapter we learn about what is class and its object. Here we can say that object is a class type variable and class is a name of type hold by object that is blueprint of object.
- We can access class variables with functions define in blueprint i.e. inside class.
- Once class is declared and define in a function by allocating memory on it, we say class is initialized to its default behavior. By doing so memory is allocated to each member variable separately of size of its type say integer holds four bytes and so other member variable.
- So total memory allocated to class is summation of all member variable type size i.e. (char (1byte) + integer (4byte)+float (4byte) + double (8byte) and array of integer is 4 * 10 size of integer array
- Member functions have allocated only once and it is shared by all objects of same class.
- .A class can be friend of another class. Such a friend class of a class has full privilege to access its members.
- A class can contain object of another class as its member then such a relationship between classes are called containership. In this one class

contains objects of some other class without "IS A" relationship. It is called "HAS A" relationship.

- Now sometimes when project gets complicated then a situation comes where class A contains class B and class B contains class A object but there is no direct relationship between then. Then it is very difficult for a class to access each other variable because of unknown variable type in class A. So we need global declaration for class B, before we write class A. Such a declaration is called forward declaration where compiler allocates memory by saying that the type class B is known in advance to compiler.

17.11 Hausaufgaben

1. Write a class HomeAutomation with panel of switch board then creates another class Lights which is a friend of HomeAutomation class and to on lights access switch ON/OFF.
2. Read more about friend classes in C++. What is there significance to application?
3. Calculate area, volume and perimeter of by writing C functions in C++ and calculate sum of sides. Consider height of pi triangle.

Chapter 18.
Class Type Function

In C++ classes are created by handling single responsibility principle methodology. To access class features class object is required. Now in C++ to initiate class object something is required and that is provided by compiler by in-built methods. In-built initialisation is made with a function called constructor by compiler of C++ language. This allows creation of object without specifying constructor in public section of class.

18.1 Constructor

In C++, constructors are used to initiate object of a particular class. If constructor is not define then compiler provides a constructor to programmer. There are different types of constructors based on parameters. Constructor name is same as class name. There classification is given below,

1. Non-Parameterise Constructor or default constructor
2. Parameterise Constructor
3. Copy Constructor
4. Default Constructor

This type of constructor have same name as class name along with it accepts no parameters as a arguments. If programmer not specify non-parameterise constructor then compiler does this for us. It invoke whenever object of class is created. But whenever there are two constructors are present i.e. default and parameterise developer explicitly needs to specify non-parameterise constructor inside class.

Example :

```
class switchBoard {
public:
        switchBoard ( ) {
        ...;
        }
```

```
        void showSwicthBoardUI ( );
    };
    void switchboard :: showSwicthBoardUI() {
        ...; }
```

2. Parameterise Constructor

This type of constructor have same name as class name but have parameters in its argument list. This constructor is used when to initialise class members with initial value. This constructor gets invoke on creation of object but argument needs to be match. when two or more constructors are specified in class it calls constructor overloading the same way as function overloading. Only difference is class name and function-name should be separate.

Example:

```
    class switchBoard {
    int buttonNo;
    string buttonName;
    public:
        // non-parameterise constructor
        switchBoard ( ) {
        ...;
        }
        // parameterise constructor
    switchBoard ( const int swButtonNo, const string
    swButtonName ) {
                buttonNo     = swButtonNo;
                buttonName = swButtonName;
        }
        void showSwicthBoardUI ( );
    };
    void switchboard :: showSwicthBoardUI() {
```

```
        ...;
}
int main ( ) {
 switchBoard Sw ( 2, "LED_2" );
Sw.showSwitchBoardUI ( );
return 0;
}
```

3. Copy Constructor

In many cases we assign local variables with global variables for local copy. In case C++ is based on OOPs methodology some ways to initiate objects of same class with one another for there local use by coping entire set of object memory. Local memory allows to manipulates information without affecting actual or global parameters. Developer can verify result in local context and later can be used or modify result into global context. To achieve same context in case of object of class we need "copy constructor" in C++. Copy constructor is function same with class name who take reference to object of same class as an argument to function. To explain this scenario consider a home automation system in customer needs to interact with digital switch board. Now to create virtual copies of switch board we need "copy constructor" in C++. In copy constructor there are two types by which copy can be made from original constructor. One method is shallow copy and other is deep copy constructor. In shallow copy both objects are pointing to same set of information. In case of deep copy both objects have different set of information in memory independently.

Syntax:

```
class class-name {
        ...;
public:
        class-name ( class-name & ) {
                ...;
                ...;
        }
};
```

Example:

```
class CopyConstructor {
public:
        CopyConstructor ( CopyConstructor &Object ) {
                ...;
        }
};
```

Constructor are very very helpful in allocating memory on heap. There is no other alternative in which allocates memory to object of a class at run time.

18.2 Call to Copy Constructor (CC)

There are many ways to call constructor of a class. If calling of copy constructor (CC) is not required but object to be initialise from another object following way is use by compiler in C++.

Syntax:

```
object-name1 = object-name2;     // no call to CC
```

In above case class name is not specified but only object-names are mentioned to avoid call to CC.

Example:

```
swicthBoardRed = swicthBoardWhite;
// no call to switch board CC
```

Syntax:

```
1. class-name object-name2 = object-name1;
// call to CC
2. class-name object-name2 ( object-name1 );
// call to CC
```

18.3 Dynamic Constructor

In small program or limited memory or temporary allocation or academic practices allocation of program resources are made on stack. Allocation on stack doesn't cause significant run-time issues. In case of large programs and permeant allocation and life cycle of application. To effectively implement and manage application memory is allocated on heap witch is quite sufficient in space. To achieve allocation we need dynamic constructor and is only option available. Dynamic constructor call is made by allocation of memory be "new" operator.

Syntax:

```
class-name object-name = new class-name;
```

Example:

```
SwitchBoard switch = new SwicthBoard;
```

18.4 Destructor In C++

To deallocates memory acquired with constructor that may be both dynamic and static, compiler provides a built-in tool function called destructor. This function too have same name as class name but preceded with tilt (~) sign. Destructor function not accept any argument or parameter for deallocation of resources. Destructor invoke as object of class goes out of scope in case of static allocation. In dynamic allocation explicitly invoke through call made to "delete" operator. In static call to destructor, deallocation of memory happens in reverse order as of allocation.

Syntax:

```
~class-name() {
        …; }
```

Example:

```
class Destructor {
        …;
public:
        Destructor ( ) {
        …;
        }
        ~ Destructor ( ) {
        …;
```

```
            // deallocates memory;
            }
    };
```

18.5 Explicit Call to Destructor

Explicit call to destructor is made by "delete" operator in C++. When memory allocation is on stack destructor of a classes are called in reverse order of creation. This is not true in case of heap allocation. Memory allocated on heap needs to be freed by giving explicit call to operator "delete". When delete invoke intern invoke destructor of respective object under deletion and frees memory allocation on heap. In such a deallocation care must be taken while freeing memory as it may happen that pointers or some part of application is requiring it and in other context deleting it. In such a case crash happened at run-time. Usually during exit of application a clean-up function is written by well known developer reducing chances of application crash. The freeing memory developer gives call to delete manually in code ensures less requirement or use of available memory.

Syntax:

```
    delete object-name;        // object of a class under clean-up
```

Example:

```
    SwitchBoard *ptrSB      = new SwitchBoard;
    delete ptrSB;     // invokes destructor of class SwitchBoard zand
            // free memory on heap.
```

18.6 Explicit Keyword In C++

In C++ there is automatic type conversion from one type to another type. To explain scenario consider that home automation system project. In that modules needs to pass LED brightness to low level code. Now if we pass integer directly, UI doesn't understand integer but shows string type. Now the question is string is not converted to int automatically and in-appropriated routine gets invoke. To avoid such a implicit promotion of variable keyword "explicit" is written to constructor usually when single argument is passes to constructor.

Example below compiles and gives output is 10. By making constructor with explicit keyword, compiler generates error since type conversion from class LEDBrightness to integer is invalid. In below code change line by adding explicit keyword shown below, *explicit* LEDBrightness (int ledBrightness) : mledBrightness (ledBrightness) { }

Example:

```
#include <iostream>
using namespace std;
class LEDBrightness {
private:
        int mledBrightness;
public:
        explicit LEDBrightness (int ledBrightness) : mledBrightness
(ledBrightness) {
        }
        int getLEDBrightness() const {
                return mledBrightness;
        }
};
void showBrightness (LEDBrightness lLED) {
        cout<<"Brightness : "<<lLED.getLEDBrightness()<<"\n";
        }
int main() {
        showBrightness(10);
        //when specified with explicit gives error.
        return 0;
}
```

Output:

```
        Brightness : 10
```

18.7 Creation and Deletion of Objects

In C++ when we create object and call its constructor, object gets memory allocation on stack memory and not on heap memory allocation because we have not use “new” operator for allocation of objects. Similarly memory allocated to objects on stack gets deallocated automatically when that particular object goes out of scope and de-allocation happens in reverse order. No need to call destructor by “delete”. This example is valid for stack memory allocation.

Example:

```
#include <iostream>

using namespace std;

class DemoConDestr {

int iobjCnt; //object tracking variable

public:

        DemoConDestr() {

        iobjCnt = 0;

        }

        DemoConDestr(int iObjCnt) {

        iobjCnt = iObjCnt;

        cout<<"Object Created : "<<iobjCnt<<endl;

        }

        ~ DemoConDestr() {

        cout<<"Object Destroyed : "<<iobjCnt<<endl;

        }

};

int main() {

        DemoConDestr obj1(1);

        DemoConDestr obj2(2);

        DemoConDestr obj3(3);

        DemoConDestr obj4(4);

        DemoConDestr obj5(5);

        return 0;
```

}

Output:

```
Object Created : 1        Object Created : 2
Object Created : 3        Object Created : 4
Object Created : 5
Object Destroyed : 5      Object Destroyed : 4
Object Destroyed : 3      Object Destroyed : 2
Object Destroyed : 1
```

18.8 Summary

- In this chapter we learn about constructor function whose name is same as class name. We can have parameterized constructor that takes arguments.
- Similarly to constructor we have destructor whose name is same as class name but preceded by tilt (~) sign. It doesn't take any argument as a parameter.
- Constructor and Destructor are used to initialize objects and destroy objects in opposite order of invocation.

18.9 Hausaufgaben

1. Create a class called HomeAutomation. Write constructor and destructor. Also proves lights are made off in opposite order of their ignition.
2. Write example to demonstrate explicit keyword.

NOTES

Chapter 19.
Inheritance C++ Feature

Inheritance is a mechanism through its use programmer or developer allowed to implement features of existing class in sub extended class or simply sub class. Basically in complex application many modules are written and should communicates with each other by message passing. To have single responsibility principle and features of extension a mechanism is introduce is called inheritance of a class. It reuses already design and tested functionality in new class from existing one is called inheritance.

19.1 Types of Inheritance

In inheritance, classification of type is completely based on hierarchical organization of classes implemented. There are only five types of hierarchical organization as below,

1. Single Inheritance
2. Multiple Inheritance
3. Multi-Level Inheritance
4. Hierarchical Inheritance
5. Hybrid inheritance

- Single Inheritance

In this there only one base or parent class and only one subclass or child class or derived class. There is no further extension from child class in application.

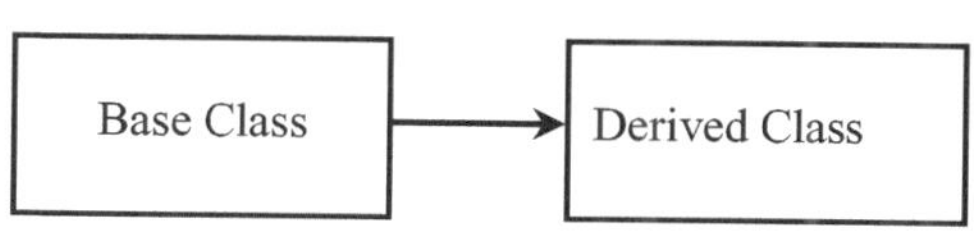

Syntax:

```
class BaseClass { };
class DerivedClass : public BaseClass { };
```

In the below example a class is derived from base class by public inheritance mode, shows single inheritance.

Example:

```
class BaseClassBrightness {
int mBrightness;
public:
        BaseClassBrightness() { }
        int getBrightness() {
        return mBrightness;
        }
        void setBrightness(int lBrightness) {
        mBrightness = lBrightness;
        }
        void showBrightness() {
        cout<<"Brightness Is = "<<mBrightness<<endl;
        }
};
class DerivedClassLEDBrightness : public BaseClassBrightness
{
int mLEDBrightness;
public:
        DerivedClassLEDBrightness() { }
        int getLEDBrightness() {
        return mLEDBrightness;
        }
```

```
        void setLEDBrightness(int lLEDBrightness) {
        mLEDBrightness = lLEDBrightness;
        }
        void showLEDBrightness() {
        cout<<"LED Brightness Is = "<<mLEDBrightness<<endl;
        }
};
int main() {
        // derived class object access base class members
        DerivedClassLEDBrightness LEDBrightness;
        LEDBrightness.setLEDBrightness(60);
        LEDBrightness.showLEDBrightness();
        LEDBrightness.setBrightness(60);
        LEDBrightness.showBrightness();
        return 0;
        }
```

- Multi-level Inheritance

In this a class are derived from respective derived class is called multi-level inheritance are present. In this two or more levels are present. In multi-level inheritance each class follows single responsibility principle of design. See figure with three blocks.

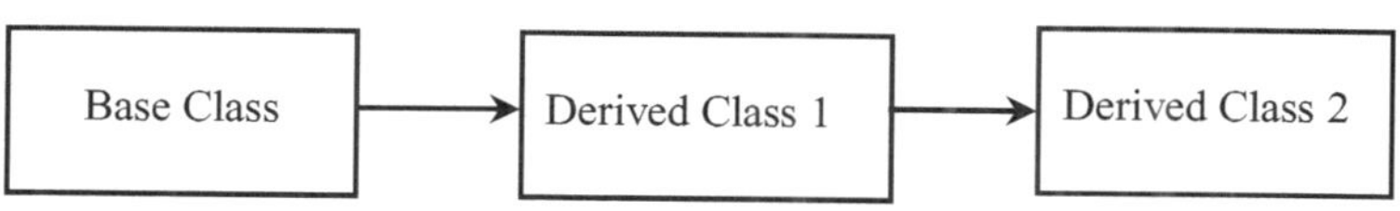

Syntax:

```
        class Brightness { };
        class LEDBrightness      : public Brightness { };
        class HallLEDBrightness : public LEDBrightness { };
```

In the example there are two levels or more levels of inheritance as shown in figure.

Example:

Example remains same as single inheritance, but just add following code snippet to this example.

```
class DerivedClassHallLEDBrightness :
        public DerivedClassLEDBrightness {
public:
        DerivedClassHallLEDBrightness() { }
        void showHallLEDBrightness() {
        cout<<"Hall LED Brightness Is = "<<getLEDBrightness()
                                    <<endl;
        }
        void setHallLEDBrightness(int lHallLEDBrightness) {
        setLEDBrightness(lHallLEDBrightness);
        setBrightness(lHallLEDBrightness);
        }
};
int main() {
        // derived class object access base class members
        DerivedClassHallLEDBrightness LEDBrightness;
        LEDBrightness.setHallLEDBrightness(60);
        LEDBrightness.showHallLEDBrightness();
        LEDBrightness.showLEDBrightness();
        LEDBrightness.showBrightness();
        return 0;
        }
```

- Multiple Inheritance

In this two or more base classes are present and only single child class derived from all base classes is called multiple inheritance. In below example three base classes are inserted by single derived class, is the example of multiple inheritance. A example of file stream classes are derived from single iOS class. and later ios class implemented by multiple inheritance way.

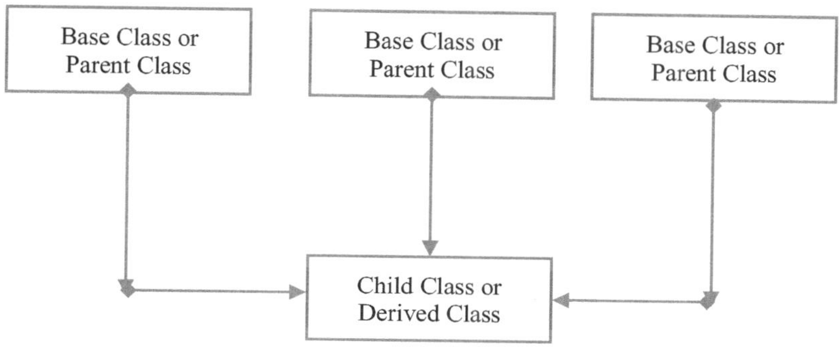

Syntax:

```
class Brightness { };
class Regulator { };
class LEDRegulator : public Brightness,
                                public Regulator { };
```

Example:

In the example below, there are two base classes and single derived class.

```
class Brightness {
public:
        void showBrightness() {
        cout<<"Brightness Shown "<<endl;
        }
};
class Regulator {
public:
        void showRegulator() {
```

```
        cout<<"Regulator Shown "<<endl;
        }
};
class LEDRegulator : public Brightness, public Regulator {
public:
        void showLEDRegulator() {
        showRegulator();
        showBrightness();
        }
};
int main() {
        LEDRegulator LEDRegulator;
        LEDRegulator.showLEDRegulator();
        return 0;
}
```

- Hierarchical Inheritance

In this single base class and multiple derived classes are present extending same base class

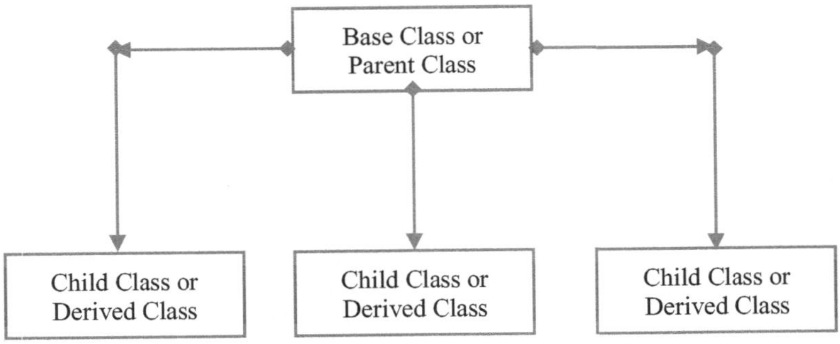

Syntax:

```
class LEDRegulator { };
class Brightness : public LEDRegulator { };
class Regulator : public LEDRegulator { };
```

Example:

In the example below, there is single base class and multiple derived classes.

```
class LEDRegulator {
public:
        LEDRegulator() { }
        void showRegulator() {
        cout<<"Regulator Shown "<<endl;
        }

        void showBrightness() {
        cout<<"Brightness Shown "<<endl;
        }
};
class Brightness : public LEDRegulator  {
public:
        Brightness() { }
        void showBrightnessOfLED() {
                showBrightness(); // base version
        }
};
class Regulator : public LEDRegulator  {
public:
        Regulator() { }
        void showRegulatorOfFan() {
                showRegulator(); // base version
        }
};
```

```
int main() {
        Brightness objBrightness;
        objBrightness.showBrightnessOfLED();
        Regulator objRegulator;
        objRegulator.showRegulatorOfFan();
        return 0;
}
```

- Hybrid Inheritance

In this type two or more types of inheritance are combined together to form a commonly called hybrid inheritance in inheritance classification. In below single, multilevel, multiple inheritances are embedded together.

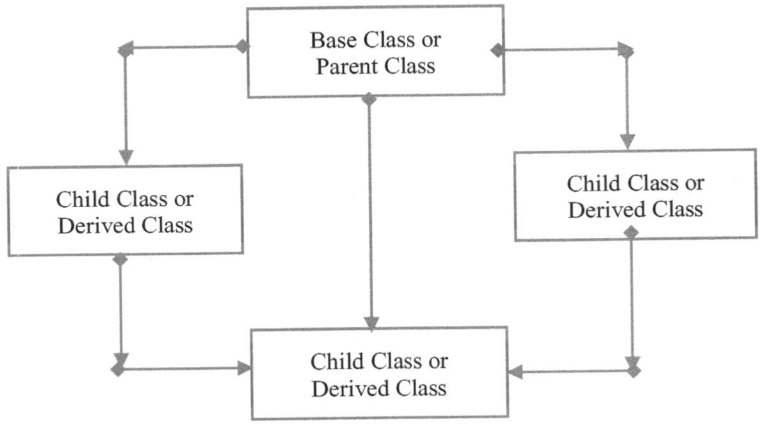

Syntax:

```
//multiple inheritance
class LEDRegulator { };
class Brightness : public LEDRegulator { };
class Regulator : public LEDRegulator { };
// multi-level inheritance
class HallLED : public Brightness { };
```

Example:

In the example, is the extension of example shown in case of hierarchical inheritance and code for multi-level inheritance is shown below. Below example is of hybrid inheritance containing multi-level and multiple inheritance together.

```
class HallLED : public Brightness {
int mLEDBrightness;
public:
        void showHallLEDBrightness () {
        showBrightness();          //base version
        cout<<"HALL LED Brightness Is = "<<mLEDBrightness
                                           <<endl;
        }
        void setHallLEDBrightness (int lLEDBrightness) {
                mLEDBrightness = lLEDBrightness;
        }
};
int main() {
        Brightness objBrightness;
        objBrightness.showBrightnessOfLED();
        Regulator objRegulator;
        objRegulator.showRegulatorOfFan(); //Multiple Inheritance

        HallLED hallLED;           //multilevel Inheritance
        hallLED.setHallLEDBrightness(60);
        hallLED.showHallLEDBrightness();
        return 0;
}
```

19.2 Define Relation between Classes

In relation with base classes and derived class, a atomic way is chosen by creator of C and C++. To define relation between classes and its access visibility mode is specified by language developer. In above syntax multiple classes are too specified by programmer.

```
class PrimeBaseClass {
                variable-names;
        public:
                function-names;
        };
```

Syntax:

```
class DerivedClassName : visibility-mode BaseClassName, visibility-mode
BaseClassName {
                variable-names;
        public:
                function-names;
        };
```

In below example illustration of single inheritance in C++ in public inheritance mode

Example:

```
        class PrimeDerivedClass : public PrimeBaseClass {
                variable-names;
        public:
                function-names;
        };
```

19.3 Defining Access Specifier For Inheritance

In inheritance specifying access represent how a particular class is visible and limits its scope in hierarchical trees of inheritance in C++. In C++ there are three

visibility modes are available. They are public, private and protected. Lets see there usage as per visibility in C++.

19.3.1 Public Visibility Mode

Public visibility mode is specified by keyword "public" before class name in inheritance path. When public is specified all public members of base class are directly accessible to derived class. Private members of base class are not at all inheritable. If developer tries to use alternate ways they are not inheritable. In public inheritance mode private members become private and public members become public in inherited class. Protected remains protected in inheritance.

19.3.2 Private Visibility Mode

Private visibility mode is specified by keyword "private" before class name in inheritance path. If not mentioned then by default it is private. When private is specified all public members of base class are not accessible to derived class. Private members of base class are not at all inheritable. If developer tries to use alternate ways they are not inheritable. In private inheritance mode private members become private and public members become private in inherited class. Protected becomes private in inheritance.

19.3.3 Protected Visibility Mode

Protected visibility mode is specified by keyword "protected" before class name in inheritance path. When protected is specified all public members of base class are directly accessible to derived class. Private members of base class are not at all inheritable. If developer tries to use alternate ways they are not inheritable. In protected inheritance mode private members become private and public members become protected in inherited class. Protected remains protected in inheritance. Protected members have limited access than public and then private members. Protected members are accessible to immediate derived class and beyond is outside its scope.

To explain above scenario consider that home automation system project. In that modules needs to be communicated with each other and programmer also wants to give user a restricted access to its information. Since private members are not inheritable in any case only option remain is protected visibility. In that members are visible to immediate derived class that it implements. Public access specifier allows full access of data members so its not desirable when restriction on data are made by programmer.

19.4 Virtual Base Class and Abstract Class

In inheritance many times it happened that same functionality existed in multiple inheritance path. Such a situation compiler and its multiple copies of respective functions are created in memory. To avoid multiple creation of copies and have unique approach to programming, requiring limited memory required less copies of objects in memory. In case of virtual base class developer ensures that single copy of data members implemented through multiple path i.e. through hybrid inheritance. In this scenario it is possible that same copies of data members are shared via multiple path. So it is advantageous have virtual base class.

Syntax:

```
class ShowDeviceStatus { };
class LEDDevice : virtual public ShowDeviceStatus { };
class RegulatorDevice : virtual public ShowDeviceStatus    { };
class DeviceStatus : public LEDDevice, public
RegulatorDevice { };
```

Example:

In the below code virtual keyword is added to resolve multiple copies of same function gets restricted in derived version of class through inheritance path.

```
class ShowDeviceStatus {
public:
        void showDeviceStatus() {
        cout<<"Device Status Successful "<<endl;
        }
};
class LEDDevice : virtual public ShowDeviceStatus {
public:
        void showLEDDeviceStatus() {
        cout<<"LED Device Status Successful "<<endl;
        }
};
```

```
class RegulatorDevice : virtual public ShowDeviceStatus {
public:
        void showRegulatorDeviceStatus() {
        cout<<"Regulator Device Status Successful "<<endl;
        }
};
class DeviceStatus : public LEDDevice, public RegulatorDevice {
public:
        //this class body is kept empty but yes you can add
        //function that you need for application
};
int main() {
        DeviceStatus led;
        led.showRegulatorDeviceStatus();
        led.showLEDDeviceStatus();
        led.showDeviceStatus();
        //this line gives error if virtual is absent in inheritance path
        return 0;
}
```

19.4.1 Abstract Class

If class is not used to create object of its own class and marked virtual in inheritance path is called abstract class in C++. Usually abstract class contains pure virtual function which doesn't allow to create or initialise its own class.

19.5 Order of Constructor Execution

In C++ when hierarchy is defined through inheritance mechanism then respective class object to be created and its data members to be initiated is proper and prior order to guarantee initialisation of objects. Orderly execution and initialisation of base class through derived class is called order of inheritance or initialisation parameter list in derived class.

19.5.1 Order of execution with different classes.

Inheritance Type	Its Order Of Execution
Single Inheritance	1. Base Class Constructor 2. Derived Class Constructor
Multiple inheritance	1. Base Class Constructor 2. Base Class Constructor (2nd) 3. Derived Class Constructor
Multiple Inheritance With Virtual Base Class	1. Virtual Base Class Constructor 2. Base Class Constructor 3. Derived Class Constructor

Syntax:

derived-class-constructor (arg1, arg2, arg3, arg4, …) : base-class-constructor (arg1) ,base-class-constructor (arg2),base-class-constructor (arg3), base-class-constructor (arg4), …

```
{
        // body of a class
};
```

Example:

```
#include <iostream>
using namespace std;
class SwitchOnLights {
        bool mKitchenLights;
        bool mHallLights;
        bool mStdudyRoomLights;
        bool mBedRoomLights;
public:
        SwitchOnLights(bool lKitchenLights,bool lHallLights,
        bool lStdudyRoomLights,bool lBedRoomLights) :
                        mKitchenLights(lKitchenLights),
                        mHallLights(lHallLights),
```

```
                mStdudyRoomLights(lStdudyRoomLights),
                mBedRoomLights(lBedRoomLights)
            {
            // initialisation list through Single Inheritance
            }
        void showLightsStatus() {
        cout<<"Kitchen Lights are On : "<<mKitchenLights<<endl;
        cout<<"Hall Lights are On : "<<mHallLights<<endl;
        cout<<"Study Room Lights are On : " <<
        mStdudyRoomLights<<endl;
        cout<<"BedRoom Lights are On :  " << mBedRoomLights
        <<endl;
        }
};
class LEDLights : public SwitchOnLights {
public :
        LEDLights() : SwitchOnLights(false,false,true,true)
        {  //Base class initialise through derived class}
};
int main() {
        LEDLights lLEDLights;
        lLEDLights.showLightsStatus();
        return 0;
}
```

Output:

```
        Kitchen Lights are On : 0
        Hall Lights are On : 0
        Study Room Lights are On : 1
```

BedRoom Lights are On : 1

19.6 Ambiguity in Inheritance

In inheritance it is quietly possible that same function name is present in multiple paths of inheritance hierarchy. To explain this scenario consider home automation system where "showDevice Status" is implemented to show status of device in multiple classes and quite possible that desired functionality is not invoke since ambiguous to resolve conflict that occurred through path. This ambiguous path is usually occurred through hybrid inheritance. In this two or more types of inheritances are possible. Say single inheritance as of now. To resolve ambiguity class-name along with scope resolution operator is used to invoke ambiguous function call.

Syntax:

```
classname::functionName();
```

Example:

```
class ShowDeviceStatus {
public:
    void showDeviceStatus() {
    cout<<"Device Status Successful "<<endl;
    }
};
class LEDDevice : public ShowDeviceStatus {
public:
    void showDeviceStatus() {
    cout<<"LED Device Status Successful "<<endl;
    }
};
int main() {
    LEDDevice led;
    led.showDeviceStatus(); // derived version
```

```
        led.ShowDeviceStatus::showDeviceStatus();
        //base version to resolve ambiguity
        return 0;
}
```

Example On Inheritance Order and Global Variable usage.

```
#include<iostream>
using namespace std;
int i = 1;
class BaseOne {
public:
        BaseOne() {
                cout<<"BaseOne\n";
        }
        ~BaseOne() {
                i=10;
                cout<<"Destructor BaseOne\n";
        }
};
class BaseTwo {
public:
        BaseTwo() {
                cout<<"BaseTwo\n";
        }
        ~BaseTwo() {
                i=11;
        out<<" DestructorTwo\n";
        }
```

```
};
class Derived : public BaseOne, public BaseTwo {
public:
        Derived() {
                cout<<"Derived\n";
        }
        ~Derived() {
                i=12;
                cout<<"Destructor\n";   }
};
int fun() {
        i = 3;
        {
                Derived d;
        }
        return i;
}
int main() {
        cout<<"i = "<<fun()<<endl;
        return 0;
}
```

Output:

```
BaseOne         BaseTwo
Derived                 Destructor
DestructorTwo           Destructor BaseOne
i = 10
```

19.7 Virtual Destructor

Consider you have a switchboard as a base class and onlights is inherited class or a derived class. Now in inheritance when developer tries to delete/free memory allocated to derived class via base class results in undefined behavior. It meaning that only base class destructor is invoked and not the derived one even base is pointing to derived object.

SwictchBoard *sb = onLights; //base points to derived object

As above statement is perfectly valid, compiler doesn't alert us about issue but skip calling destrcuctor version of derived class.

Example:

```
class SwicthBoard {
public:
   SwicthBoard() {
                cout<<"\nSwitchBoard Created\n";
            cout<<"Lights are turned ON.";
   }
   ~SwicthBoard() {
          cout<<"\nLights are turned OFF.";
          cout<<"SwitchBoard Destroyed\n";
   }
};
class onLights : public SwicthBoard {
public:
   onLights() {
          cout<<"\n onLights Created\n";
          cout<<"Switching Lights ON."<<endl;
   }
   ~onLights() {
          cout<<"\n Lights are turned off"<<endl;
```

```
        cout<<"onLights Object Deleted"<<endl;
    }
};
int main() {
        SwicthBoard *sb;
        onLights *ols = new onLights;
        sb = ols;
        delete sb;
return 0;
}
```

Output:

SwitchBoard Created

Lights are turned ON.

onLights Created

Switching Lights ON.

Lights are turned OFF.

SwitchBoard Destroyed //base version and no derivedone

Remeady to above problem is to make base version of destructor as a virtual destructor function by writing "virtual" as shown in below example.

Example:

```
virtual ~SwicthBoard() {
      cout<<"\nLights are turned OFF.";
      cout<<"SwitchBoard Destroyed\n";
   }
```

Output:

SwitchBoard Created

Lights are turned ON.

onLights Created

Switching Lights ON.

Lights are turned off

onLights Object Deleted   //called derived version

Lights are turned OFF.

SwitchBoard Destroyed // called base version

19.8 Initialization list of Class

Initialization list is a sequence of parameter passed to a class constructor to initialize its member prior initialization of class. It is must to follow order in base class declaration. First declared variable in base class must be initialized first and then second declared and so on upto last declared member variable.

This kind of ideology prevents and control initialization of base class parameters.

Example:

```
class InitBase {
   char *ch_ptr;
   int first;
   float second;
   string strBaseClassName;
public:
   InitBase (int lFirst, char *lch_prt,float lSecond):
         ch_ptr(lch_prt),
         first(lFirst),
         second(lSecond),
         strBaseClassName("InitBase"){
   }
   void showInitialization() {
      cout<<"ch_ptr size = "<<string(ch_ptr).length()<<endl;
      cout<<"ch_ptr  = "<<string(ch_ptr)<<endl;
      cout<<"int first = "<<first<<endl;
```

```
        cout<<"float second = "<<second<<endl;
        cout<<"Base class name = "<<strBaseClassName<<endl;
    }
    ~InitBase() {
        cout<<"\nObject Destroyed\n";
    }
};
int main() {
char *strId = new char[5];
    strId[0] = 'L';
    strId[1] = 'E';
    strId[2] = 'D';
    strId[3] = '0';
    strId[4] = '1';

InitBase *initclass = new InitBase(10,strId,100.10);
    initclass->showInitialization();
    delete []strId;
    delete initclass;
}
```

Output:

```
        ch_ptr size = 5
        ch_ptr = LED01
        int first = 10
        float second = 100.1
        Base class name = InitBase
        Object Destroyed
```

19.9 Custom Class Design (string class)

How to design own custom class for particular implementation say to design our own custom string class.

Example:

```
#include<iostream>
#include<string>
using namespace std;
class QCustomString : public string {
public:
    QCustomString() : string() {}
    QCustomString(const QCustomString &str) : string(str) {}
    QCustomString operator + (const QCustomString &str) const {
    QCustomString result(*this);
        result += str;
        return result;
    }
    QCustomString(const string &str) : string(str) {}
    friend ostream& operator<<(ostream &out, const QCustomString &str)   {
        out << static_cast<const string&>(str);
        return out;
    }
};
int main() {
    QCustomString t_company("Embitel");
    QCustomString t_employee("Shetye Girish");
    QCustomString employee = t_company + " " + t_employee;
    cout << employee << endl;
    return 0;
}
```

19.10 Summary

- In this chapter, we learn about inheritance and its types as single, multiple, multilevel, hybrid and hierarchical.
- We learn about how to specify inheritance syntax, access specifiers such as public, private and protected and their visibility and use.
- We learn about what is mean by virtual base class and its significance on inheritance. It prevents multiple copies from inheritance.
- We learn about abstract base class and its use.

19.11 Hausaufgaben

1. Write with example what do you mean by inheritance and its type. Why they required or how these technique simplifies developer work.
2. Explain different access specifiers and how they can be used to control visibility of class with respect to another inherited class.
3. What is mean by ambiguity in inheritance and how it controlled with virtual classes? Give example.

Chapter 20.

Operator Overloading In C++

In operator overloading technique, operation is performed on user-defined type as the same way as built-in operator performs on user information. To explain this scenario consider a home automation system in customer needs to interact with digital switch board to turn off all lights or turn off few lights by changing individual status associated with it. To achieve mentioned functionality, suppose there are ten LED lights are present numbered from one to ten respectively. Before going to sleep each night LED number one, three, seven and nine must remain ON and rest are put off. This to be achieve with single digital switch by customer. A developer inverts sign associated with such a object rather individual variables associated with LED switch. Operator overloading is essential task that reduces handling individual role by giving opportunity to object to perform like built-in type by use of operator overloading feature in C++. Or before shutdown of home automation application inverting all members if not inverted is a task of operator function and safely closing application. Operator overloading normally take object as a argument to operator function. Or you can invert individual object as it is matter of implementation how a developer use this feature. It is based on how you comfortable with this.

20.1 Operator Overloading Function

Syntax:

```
return-type class-name : : operator operator-symbol ( arg1, arg2, …) {
        function-body;
}
```

Example:

```
void SwitchBoard :: operator — () {
        LED1 =  - LED1;
        LED2 =  - LED2;
}
```

20.2 Rules For Operator Overloading (OO)

1. Operator Function is either member function or friend function.
2. Overloading unary operator through use of member function takes no argument while through friend function takes one arguments. Since unary operator works with single or no arguments.
3. Overloading binary operator through use of member function takes one argument while through friend function takes two arguments. Since binary operator works with single or two arguments at a time.
4. Scope Resolution (: :), conditional operator (?:) operator can't be overloaded as it is prohibited from it.
5. " sizeof " operator can't be overloaded as it is prohibited from it.
6. membership operator (.) and pointer to member (.*) operator can't be overloaded as it is prohibited from it.
7. In OO, new operator cannot be created. Only existing are use and overloaded by OO technique.
8. Original meaning of operator are not changed even after overloading of operator i.e. unary operators are not used as binary operator. Operator plus (+) can't be used for subtraction of two values as it loses original meaning.
9. There are few operator are overloaded without use of friend keyword. They must not use friend keyword to overload then are as follows,
    1. Subscript Operator ([ ])
    2. Assignment Operator (=)
    3. Member Access Operator (—>)
    4. Function Call Operator (())

20.3 Example Of OO unary minus (-) sign

```
class SwitchBoard {
        int LED1;
        int LED2;
public:
        SwitchBoard () {
```

```
                LED1 = 0;
                LED2 = 0;
        }
        void switchLEDOn () {
                LED1 = 1;
                LED2 = 1;
        }
        void operator - ();
        void showLEDStatus () {
        cout<<"LED1 =  "<<LED1<<"\n";
        cout<<"LED2 =  "<<LED2<<"\n";
        }
};
void SwitchBoard :: operator - () {          //unary operator overload
                LED1 = - LED1;
                LED2 = - LED2;
        }
int main () {
        SwitchBoard sb;
        sb.switchLEDOn();
        sb.showLEDStatus();
        -sb; // LEDs status changes
        sb.showLEDStatus();
        return 0;
}
```

20.4 Overloading binary operator plus (+)

In this example two different sets (setOne and setTwo) of LEDs are added together like adding two integers directly. Assume that set one is of red colour and set two is of yellow colour.

```
class SwitchBoard {
int totalLEDs;
public:
	SwitchBoard() {
		totalLEDs = 0;
	}
	explicit SwitchBoard(int iLEDs):totalLEDs(iLEDs) {
	}
	SwitchBoard & operator + (SwitchBoard &objSB);
	void showTotalLEDs() {
	cout<<"Total LEDs On are : "<<totalLEDs<<endl;
	}
};
SwitchBoard& SwitchBoard :: operator + (SwitchBoard &objSB) {
	this->totalLEDs += objSB.totalLEDs;
	return *this;
}
int main() {
	SwitchBoard objLEDSetOne(5);
	objLEDSetOne.showTotalLEDs();

	SwitchBoard objLEDSetTwo(5);
	objLEDSetTwo.showTotalLEDs();
```

```
        SwitchBoard showTotalLEDs = objLEDSetOne +
                                objLEDSetTwo;
        //adding two objects like integers
        showTotalLEDs.showTotalLEDs();
        return 0;
}
```

Output:

Total LEDs On are : 5

Total LEDs On are : 5

Total LEDs On are : 10

20.5 Overloading input (>>) and output (<<) stream operators

In the example, input and output streams are overloaded to “cin" and “cout" stream objects to behave directly on class objects like primitive one or built-in type.

```
class OverloadStreams {
        int LEDs;
public:
        OverloadStreams() {
                LEDs = 0;
        }
        OverloadStreams(int iLEDStreamData) {
                LEDs = iLEDStreamData;
        }
        friend ostream& operator<<(ostream& os, const
                OverloadStreams& objOStreams);
        friend istream& operator>>(istream& is,
        OverloadStreams& objInStream);
};
ostream& operator<<(ostream& os, const OverloadStreams& objOStreams) {
```

```
        os<<"LEDs OutStream = "<<objOStreams.LEDs<<endl;
        return os;
}
istream& operator>>(istream& is, OverloadStreams& objInStream) {
        //write your own example like reading from cin object
        //just mentioned as "(is>>"Enter LEDs :
                                        ">>objInStream.LEDs)"
        return is;
}
int main() {
        OverloadStreams outputStream(10);
        cout<<outputStream;
        //In the above example code snippet is given to output //LEDs Streams
        return 0;
}
```

Output:

LEDs OutStream = 10

20.6 Summary

- In this chapter we learn about operator overloading and its rules to implement it. Overloading an operator means developer performs arithmetic directly on objects with help of operator () function.
- You can overload all the operators except few that are reserved and few without taking changing its original behavior.
- Overloading unary operator takes single as that of binary operator takes two arguments. Binary operator needs friend function to perform overloading task.

20.7 Hausaufgaben

1. Practice overloading unary operator such as ++ and --.

2. Practice overloading binary operator + and – with friend and without friend functions.
3. Overload new and delete operator.
4. Specify all the operator overloading rules.
5. Specify reserved operators and why they are reserved.

NOTES

Chapter 21

Multiple Forms in C++ (Polymorphism)

In C++, polymorphism plays important role as same name can be used for multiple purpose. Also it achieves dynamic binding that transfers calls to respective procedure with same name present in multiple modules. In multiple forms, it is very important to select respective procedure depending on its type at run time. To explain this scenario consider a home automation system in customer needs to interact with digital switch board to turn off/on all lights or turn off few lights by changing individual status associated with it and similar devices. Now these switches are present in different modules of application and depending on type of module invoked application have to call "switchOffOn" function of respective module invoked by customer. So "switchOffOn" is present in multiple modules say regulator, TV, LED lights, AC, KitchenEquipments and so on. Polymorphism is best way to deal with such a programming difficulties in application.

Polymorphism is a way of selecting same name for doing multiple things in application is called polymorphism. Basically poly is term used to represent multiple forms and morphism is term used to represent multiple behaviour of those multiple forms. In OOPs polymorphism is mainly known for dynamic bindings than static bindings. It is classified in two ways in programming environment. One type of polymorphism is function and operator overloading. This is called compile time or static or early binding polymorphism. Second type of polymorphism is called late or dynamic or run time binding in which call made to procedure is known after execution of application. This is called rum time polymorphism. Runtime binding is achieved with the help of virtual functions in C++.

21.1 Types of Polymorphism

1. Static Or Compile and
2. Dynamic Or Runtime polymorphism.

21.2 Need of V-Table

In this chapter we are discussing only about dynamic polymorphism. To achieve this functionality at run time in C++ provides a keyword called "virtual". This keyword helps in resolving function call at runtime by executing binary and with the help of V-Table mechanism.

Application maintains V-Table per each class when virtual functions are defined in class. This table have mapping of virtual functions present in respective class in which functions are define. In v-table contains all the virtual functions accessible by class and pointer to there definitions. So whenever virtual functions are define compiler generates or collects two things about such a class. One is v-ptr is a pointer to function and list of functions to that v-ptr. Virtual function pointer variable is called "v-ptr" and table that contains list of all virtual function definition accessible to that class is called virtual table or simply v-table. When object of particular class requesting for function called first v-ptr is initialised with the address of function from v-table and call to function of respective class is selected on initialise or to select accessible function. This is done dynamically by executable whenever called made to virtual functions.

Virtual Functions VTable.

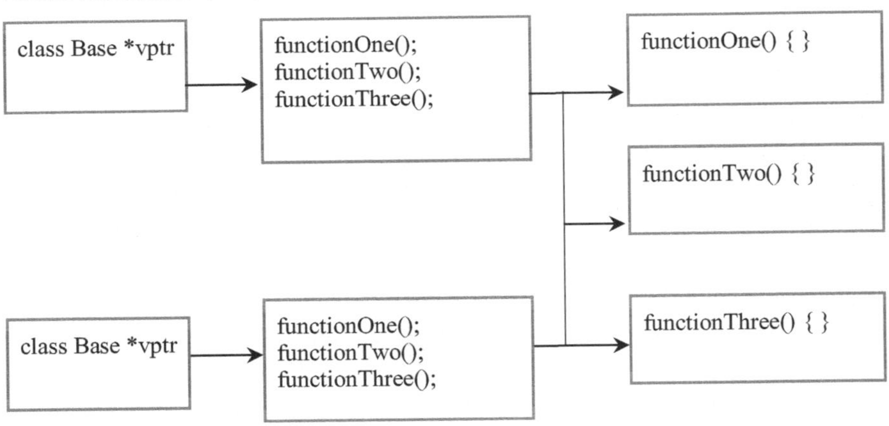

Example:

Virtual functions are required to resolve function call with the help v-ptr and v-table to achieve dynamic bindings or polymorphism in C++.

21.3 Virtual Functions

In virtual functions pointer to object of base class is used to point pointer to object of derived class and capable to invoke derived method of class that base class pointer object is pointing. This can be resolved by making base function virtual in base class.

Example:

```
class SwicthBoard {
public:
        int LED;
        SwicthBoard() {
                LED = 0;
        }
        virtual void showLEDStatus() {
                cout<<"Switch Board Initial Status,\nLED = 0\n";
        }
};
class Regulator : public SwicthBoard {
public:
        Regulator() {
                LED = 1;
        }
        void showLEDStatus() {
                cout<<"Regulatpr LED is On.\nLED = 1\n";
        }
};
class TubeLight : public SwicthBoard {
public:
        TubeLight() {
```

```
                LED = -1;
        }
        void showLEDStatus() {
                cout<<"Tubelight LED is Off.\nLED = -1\n";
        }
};
int main() {
        // base class initialisation
        SwicthBoard *ptrSwicthBoard = new SwicthBoard;
        ptrSwicthBoard->showLEDStatus();
        //base class is pointing to derived class i.e. Regulator.                //
inform base to point derived class
        ptrSwicthBoard = new Regulator;
// calling derived method through base pointer
        ptrSwicthBoard->showLEDStatus();
        //base class is pointing to derived class i.e. TubeLight
        // inform base to point derived class
        ptrSwicthBoard = new TubeLight;
        // calling derived method through base pointer
        ptrSwicthBoard->showLEDStatus();
        return 0;
}
```

21.4 Pure Virtual Functions

We seen the importance of virtual functions in dynamic bindings. So whenever we write virtual function developer has to define its body in code without that compiler throws error message. Basically virtual functions are define in base class and that base class is abstract if we do not create object of its own class. This indicates that base class with virtual function definition are comparatively not necessary in programming world without that also run-time polymorphism is possible. To implement this pure virtual functions are important as the only have prototype as header and body is not required to define functions. Virtual functions are used to resolve anomalies that come to resolve derived class pointer through base class point to object technique. Remedy to it is use pure virtual function as they act as a placeholder in base class. In example below SwitchBoard is called pure virtual function class and can not be instantiated because of pure virtual function of pure abstract class.

To explain this scenario consider a home automation system in customer needs to interact with digital switch board to turn off/on all lights or turn off few lights by changing individual status associated with it and similar devices. Better way to implement this situation in C++ to have abstract base class with pure virtual function define with "switchOff" and "switchOn" as two pure virtual functions in base class. Now the class required service from base class will implement Off/On functionality in respective module and switch off/on lights of respective device providing service.

Syntax:

```
return-type virtual function-name () = 0;
```

Example:

```
virtual void showLEDStatus() = 0;
// pure virtual function
class SwicthBoard {
public:
        int LED;
        SwicthBoard() {
                LED = 0;
        }
        virtual void showLEDStatus() = 0;
        // pure virtual function
};
class Regulator : public SwicthBoard {
public:
        Regulator() {
```

```
            LED = 1;
        }
        void showLEDStatus() {
        cout<<"Regulatpr LED is On.\nLED = 1\n";
        }
};
class TubeLight : public SwicthBoard {
public:
        TubeLight() {
                LED = -1;
        }
        void showLEDStatus() {
                cout<<"Tubelight LED is Off.\nLED = -1\n";
        }
};
int main() {
        SwicthBoard *ptrSwicthBoard =  new Regulator;
        // No base object creation
        ptrSwicthBoard->showLEDStatus();

        ptrSwicthBoard = new TubeLight;
        ptrSwicthBoard->showLEDStatus();
        return 0;
}
```

21.5 Criteria for Having Virtual Functions

1. Virtual functions are invoked with pointer to object of class
2. Virtual function cannot be a static function, can't be friend of another class

3. Virtual function must be member of class and must be implemented in servicing class.
4. We can have virtual destructor but not the constructor.
5. Virtual function defined in parent class need not be necessarily redefine in child classes.
6. In case of virtual function, prototype must be matched if not will be considered as overloaded function.
7. In virtual functions, base class can points to derived object but derived object can't points to base properties. That means derived to base is not possible.
8. Base can point to immediate derived class object and not to next class in hierarchy.

21.6 This Pointer

"this" pointer is implicitly passed to invoking function to distinguish between local and class member variables when have variable name common in between them. "this" pointers returns invoking class object of current class context. In the below example change "this->number" to only "number" and run whole program again. You will be clear about "this" pointer.

Example:

```
class ThisPointer {
        int sum;
        int number;
public:
        ThisPointer() {
                sum = 0;
                number = 0;
        }
        void add(int number) {
        // change "this->number" to "number" and run again
        sum = sum + this->number + number;
        }
```

```
        void showSum() {
        cout<<"Sum = "<<sum<<"\n";
        }
};
int main() {
        ThisPointer thp;
        thp.add(10);
        thp.showSum();
        thp.add(10);
        thp.showSum();
        return 0;
}
```

21.7 Summary

- In this chapter we learn about polymorphism and virtual functions and v-table and its use by compiler.
- We learn about static and dynamic polymorphisms i.e. compile time and run time polymorphism.
- We learn about “this” pointer which automatically passed to member function to distinguish member variable and local variable.

21.8 Hausaufgaben

1. Write a virtual method draw() in class that draws shapeOfAnimal(int animalId) which draws actual shape of animal i.e. 1.drawShapeOfDog() 2.drawShapeOfCat() and finally 3.drawShapeOfElephant(). Use dynamic polymorphism.

   Dog has animal Id = 1; Cat has animal Id = 2;

   Elephant has animal Id = 3.

   enum Animal{ANIMAL_DOG_ID, ANIMAL_CAT_ID,

   ANIMAL_ELEPHANT_ID}
2. Write an example that demonstrates this pointer.

Chapter 22.
Exception Handling In C++

In exception handling technique, there are certain events are occurring in application. Some situations are handled at OS level as it is also one form of application such as memory violation, network signal corruption, limited memory available for allocation as many applications are using storage, stack corruption by application etc. Sometimes SMS, EMAIL, News notification are required on notification bar, weather forecasting etc. Some situations like emergency services. All those are received from OS services to application. These notifications are received by OS services by implementing it in application. Next step is that application process it and without interrupting existing functionality of application background code forward it to UI of application to notify user. Best way to implement such a service of notification can be done by exception handling techniques in C++. This throwing of exception from one place directly come to UI by carrying message and UI modules notifies it on UI along with animation if interested. With this technique it is very easy to manage with complicated software architectures.

To explain this scenario, consider a home automation system in customer needs to interact with digital switch board to decrease intensity of LED lights. Now there is digital option available. This digital option updates UI as well as sends values to decrease/increase LED light intensity on actual LED lights. As actual value changes or volume of laptop speaker increase/decreases by key on laptop keyboard that value is use to update on UI along with actual increase/decrease in speaker volume. This passage of message to UI is a notification technique and information related to sound i.e. number send to UI module using exception technique as it is best way to handle it. Also, Yes/No type situation in applications is handled by throwing exception in application. Another example in embedded application is of fuel tank monitoring. If fuel in fuel tank goes below certain level, then sensor gives interrupt to application then application throws exception to notify UI and finally end user to indicate decrease in fuel level on fuel indicator in today's automobile on digital indicator.

22.1 Try and Catch Block

To implement notification or run-time error handling, C++ provides two blocks one is called try block and another is called catch block. Together it is called try catch mechanism in exception handling technique. this technique is very useful in handling dynamic issue occurred during application execution and notification. There are two types of exceptions to occur in program. One is generated by system API and other one is by application system. Both exceptions are possible to capture with this technique. In both case exception is thrown by "throw" mechanism with throw keyword. Exception is thrown by try block with the help of throw and it is catch by catch block that matches more accurately to exception type. Application have nested try catch block. Inner try block throws exception that is catch by catch block of matching type. Later in tern catch block re-throw to outer try catch block. In this way exception propagates from one module to another module of software design architecture. Noticing UI is easy with this mechanism of handling errors.

Syntax:

```
try {
        …;
        throw "exception";
}
catch ( type of exception ) {
        // handling exception or notify UI about exception
}
```

Syntax:

```
try {
        …;
        throw "exception";
}
catch ( type-of-exception1 ) {
        // handling exception or notify UI about exception
}
```

```
catch ( type-of-exception2 ) {
        // handling exception or notify UI about exception
}
```

In exception handling most matching exception block catches exception. To implement exception handling coder have to include <exception> header file. There are standard exception provided by exception class in C++.

22.2 Standard Exception from Exception Class

Standard Exceptions	Exception Explanation
bad_alloc	bad allocation exception is thrown by new whenever there is insufficient memory on heap.
bad_cast	This exception occurs whenever there is improper cast due to dynamic_cast operator
Exception	This is parent class in exception handling mechanism and use to implement custom exception scenarios in c++
bad_exception	This exception is used to handle uncertain exceptions
domain_error	This exception is used to handle invalid domain related to domain
logic_error	This exception is used to handle logic related exceptions
bad_typeid	This exception is used to handle exception thrown by typeid used to identify name of class used by developer as specially required during inheritance mechanism to type cast object of particular class
invalid_argument	This exception is used to handle exception caused by invalid argument mention to a particular function
lenght_error	This exception is used to handle exception caused by length of string mentioned as buffer is limited to hold comparatively large string
runtime_error	This exception is used to handle exception that caused at runtime by application or from system error
out_of_range	This exception is used to handle exception caused by at(i) method in c++.
overflow_error	This exception is used to handle when MSB bit is lost due to insufficient buffer size.
underflow_error	This exception is used to handle underflow issue caused in maths
range_error	This exception is used to handle exception when value of particular type is use to store in limited or smaller buffer

22.3 Define Custom Exceptions

To define custom exception developer must extends exception class as a base class and perform public inheritance with defining derived class as subclass to implement custom exception class. This custom class override what () method call and throw custom exception.

Example:

```
#include <exception>

class CustomException : public exception {

public:

        const char * what() const throw () {

                return "\nDivision By Zero Error\n";

        }

};

int main() {

        try {       // try catch block

                int divisor = 0;

                if( divisor == 0)  {

                throw CustomException();  // exception thrown

                }

        }

        catch (exception &e)  { // catch block catches exception

                cout<<e.what(); // retrieve exception thrown by try
                        block

        }

        return 0;

}
```

22.4 Throw Specific Exception

Rather catching generalise exception catch block, its better to handle individual exception to notify UI about particular event a specifying specific exception is much more better way to deal with issue that occurred executing application.

Syntax:

```
return-type function-name (arg1, arg2,...) const throw (type1, type2,...) {
    ... body;
}
```

Example:

```
class CustomException : public exception {
string strCustomException;
public:
    CustomException(string lstrCustomException) :
    strCustomException ( lstrCustomException ) {
    }
    const char * what() const throw () {
        return strCustomException.c_str();
    }
    virtual ~CustomException() throw() {
        strCustomException = "";
    }
};
int main() {
    try {
        int number = 100;
        int division = 0;
        if(division == 0) {
```

```
            throw CustomException("\nDivision By Zero Error
                    \n");
            }
    }
    catch (exception &e) {
            cout<<e.what();
    }
    return 0;
}
```

22.5 To Catch All Exception

In order to have issue less application all issues must be address or handled by application. To handle any exception that is not handled by application is handled by catch (...) block with three dot in bracket. This avoids run-time crash in application due to unhanded criteria.

Syntax:

```
    try {
            ...;
    } catch (int number)  {
    } catch (double number)  {
    }
     catch ( . . . )  { //catches any exception other than specified
            // executes only when other than int and double            //
type is thrown by try  block
    }
```

22.6 Summary

- In this chapter we learn about exception handling and how to use exception. There are two try and catch keywords are defined for this.

- In try {…} catch (exception e) {…}, In try block we write code to throw particular exception like "divide by 0", "not a number" etc. These anomalies are caught by catch () {} block.
- This exception handling technique of handling anomalies in code prevent application from crashing at run-time.
- Sometimes alert can be generated by exception handling mechanism.

22.7 Hausaufgaben

1. Write an example of traffic light controller based on traffic. When there is no traffic say "Go at 80". Turn signal into GREEN. Then wait for timer to stop and show STOP in Red COLOR and wait to another pass. CHANGE SIGNAL COLOR Orange.
2. Implement above example using exception handling at run-time for local train system. List down all possible failures and alert (fire/low oxygen/temperature) mechanism for local train/metro.

NOTES

Chapter 23
Template In C++

Template is a feature only available to C++ language and its not supported in C language. Template is a way of generic programming where code replacement task is given to compiler instead of developer or coder. In template it is responsibility of compiler to provide appropriate definition to template code written by programmer. By looking at template compiler generates appropriate definition to multiple datatypes such as int, char, float, double etc for which template is written. This kind of way of writing code with the help of compiler is called generic programming. Generic programming is a way to respond multiple datatype by writing common logic or program that responds it. To explain this scenario considers a home automation system in customer needs to interact with digital switch board to switch on/off by on/off methods. Now these methods have common way of on and off switch. To implement on and off for TV, Regulator, LED lights, music system one can implement templates or try using generic code for on/off module facilitating on/off functionality. By using templates compiler generated code for each TV, Regulator, LED lights on/off facility. In some case to perform operation on heterogeneous set of data by common logic such as sorting, comparing, swapping and displaying information template or generic coding is a great help to developer by compiler. Template also called as parameterized classes or functions.

23.1 Function Template

Function template is a generic way to write function with help of compiler by specifying common logic is called nothing but function template. Two keywords used are "template" and "typename". Template specifies name of template and typename specifies generic type for heterogeneous data. To specify type "class / typename" keywords are used.

Syntax:

template < typename lTypename>

lTypename function-name (lTypename ltype-name,

lTypename ltype-name)

```
{
        // body of a function
        return type-name;
}
```

Example:

```
        typedef int TV;              // int is defined as TV
        typedef char LED;            // char is defined as LED
        template < typename temp>          // template function
        temp MaxComaprision(temp lNoOne, temp lNoTwo) {
        temp lNo = ((lNoOne > lNoTwo) ? lNoOne : lNoTwo);
        return lNo;
  }
int main() {
        cout<<"Greater Value Switch Off TV Is "<<
                MaxComaprision<TV>(99,100)<<endl;
        cout<<"Greater Value Switch On LED  Is "<<
        MaxComaprision<LED>('C','B')<<endl;
        return 0;
}
```

In the above example "MaxComaprision" is a template function with two arguments of same type as said in TV or LED type. Same set of code or generic code is used for two different data set to turn on/off on switch board.

Another example is of sorting information by various sorting algorithms on data set. Suppose AI algorithm is used to identify different objects through camera modules best describes template methodology or how generic code helps and simplify developer work and efforts.

23.2 Function Template with Heterogenous Argument List

Many times it is required that function template needs two arguments of different set of information, following syntax have been used by programmer.

Syntax:

```
template < typename lTypenameOne, typename lTypenameTwo>
lTypename function-name ( lTypenameOne ltype-name,
                          lTypenameTwo ltype-name) {
                     // body of a function
                     return type-name;
          }
```

Example:

In heterogeneous type of template function, to explain this scenario consider a home automation system in customer needs to identify with digital camera different objects that passes through connected camera modules. Consider that camera give bulgars alarm to customer mobile by analysing objects and situation by camera module. In medical and chemical industry object can be analysed by looking at object through image processing module of camera.

23.3 Template Classes

Template classes are similar to template functions with a difference that classes are more general to information and there features whereas template functions are specific to information. If you group many features by template functions of different logic on same set of data. Template classes operates on set of data with its operational functionality is specified in generic way.

Syntax:

```
template <class T>
class class-name {
        // member variables of type T
        // T is a generic type of template type specified
        // class functions / template functions
};
// call made to template class
class-name <type-name> object-name (arg1, arg2, ...);
```

Example:

To explain this class template scenario consider a situation in customer wants to perform multiple logic operation on same or multiple set of information. Consider a home automation system in which on/off, increase/reduce volume, speed of LED, TV/Radio/Music and FAN regulator respectively. To implement above functionality a single generic class is written by programmer. Later compiler provides definition for these generic class by looking at type of data set for operation by class.

Similarly add, subtract, multiply, sorting, swapping and displaying are functionality define in generic way of particular template class in C++.

Example:

```
#include <iostream>
#include <string>
using namespace std;
template <class T>
class Calculator {
        T mItemOne;
        T mItemTwo;
public:
        Calculator() {
        }
        Calculator (T lItemOne, T lItemTwo) {
        mItemOne = lItemOne;
        mItemTwo = lItemTwo;
        }
        T addItems() {
        T lTempItem;
        lTempItem = mItemOne + mItemTwo;
        return lTempItem;
        }
```

```
        T subItems() {
        T lTempItem;
        lTempItem = mItemOne - mItemTwo;
        return lTempItem;
        }
        T multiplyItems() {
        T lTempItem;
        lTempItem = mItemOne * mItemTwo;
        return lTempItem;
        }
        void setItems (T lItemOne, T lItemTwo) {
                mItemOne = lItemOne;
                mItemTwo = lItemTwo;
        }
        void display() {
        cout<<"Item One : "<<mItemOne<<endl;
        cout<<"Item Two : "<<mItemTwo<<endl;
        }
};
int main()
{
        Calculator <int> calIntObject (10,20);
        calIntObject.display();
        cout<<"Addition Of Integers is " << calIntObject.addItems()
                        <<endl;
        calIntObject.setItems (40,60);
        calIntObject.display();
```

```
    cout<<"Addition Of Integers is "<<callIntObject.addItems()
                                    <<endl;


    Calculator <string> calStrObject ("Shetye"," Girish");
    calStrObject.display();
    cout<<"Addition Of String is "<<calStrObject.addItems()
                        <<endl;


    callIntObject.setItems (40,60);
    callIntObject.display();
    cout<<"Substraction Of Integers is "<<
    callIntObject.subItems()<<endl;
    return 0;
}
```

23.4 Template Classes with Heterogenous Arguments

In template class some time required to perform same logic operation on different set of information. Such a need of developer is fulfilled with template classes with heterogenous argument type.

Syntax:

```
template <class T1, class T2>
class class-name {
// class with type T1 and T2 are of heterogenous type
// body of class
};
```

Example is similar with above specification but needs two heterogenous argument to be specified as below

```
class-name <type1,type2> object-name (arg1, arg2); // prototype for template class
Calculator <int, float> calcObject (10, 20.55);
```

// call to template class function

23.5 Overloading Template Functions

Template functions can be overloaded like normal function overloading technique by specifying template argument and specific argument to template functions. Preference is given to non template function over template function of matching prototype.

Example:

```
template < typename temp>        // template function
        temp MaxComparison(temp lNoOne, temp lNoTwo) {
                temp lNo = ((lNoOne > lNoTwo) ? lNoOne :
                                                lNoTwo);
                return lNo;
}
        //non-template function
        int MaxComparison( int  lNoOne, int lNoTwo) {
                int lNo = ((lNoOne > lNoTwo) ? lNoOne : lNoTwo);
                return lNo;
}
```

Rules:

1. Preference is given to specialize function of matching prototype over template function.
2. Second preference given to template function of matching type
3. You can pass non-template arguments to template functions

23.6 Summary

- In this chapter we learn about function template, class template and heterogeneous argument to template. In template we write generic class or function that can be applicable to heterogeneous data type.

- Templates function or classes are replacing by its actual parameter by compiler and instead of calling generic version, its actual function with appropriate arguments invoked at run-time.
- Template can be specialize one too rather than generic one.
- We can overload templatized function in C++.

23.7 Hausaufgaben

1. Write a templatized function to perform operation such as addition, subtraction, multiplication and division. Use only single templatized function.
2. Write templatized class for above specification.
3. Overload template to find sorting of information like integer array, float array and strings i.e. array of character.

Chapter 24
Working With Files in C++

In digital world or simply in computer world information saves in electronic format. Generally we call it as file or more specifically electronic form of file in digital or computer world. Most of the time information processing, analysing and storage and transfer from one media to another is made available in electronic form of file. Electronic form of file is required for easy manipulation, reading, maintaining information in e-file (electronic file) format. There are different types of files are created with digital file systems. One is used for programming purpose, database file for maintaining records, writing novels or story books, creating audio/video content for books, creating varieties of books and so on. To create files customer need certain application to avail these features related to file system. These apps used for file handling are designed in C++ language as a middle application layer.

To explain this scenario considers a home automation system in customer needs to interact with digital switch board to switch on/off by on/off methods. But at some points on/off functionality does not give required output. if we press ON on home automation panel gives garbage results. Now at this stage we have complete system working but because of life-cycle it fails somehow. In complex embedded system it is very inconvenient to analyse complete project rather to handle this at specific point of issue. Developer needs to find what went wrong where and how. Answer to this where and how is to use records generated in working functionality and not working functionality i.e. needs comparison between working and damage systems. For these issues we have file logging system running in background. These files are in e-form (electronic form). As printers are available can gives physical copies after printing are much easier than writing on paper directly.

To create files and maintain it customer need application through it can manage all files related operations. Files required to write such a applications are written in text editor provided by filesystem supported by OS or by embedded application. Example is system.log file as it collects system related operation by writing to system.log file. Such a file can be used to track failure of operation in application and to take corrective action by knowing failures by looking into system.log file. Now a days debug generated file is used to find out exact issue logged during execution of application. This is called dump generation on failure of application which also prevent crash and on restart we can re-run our application. Later this debug file is used to find out exact issue logged for particular exception. This debug is submitted and may be online and problems are diagnosed by developer of app.

24.1 File Streams

In file handling we need connection between application and file and file to application. To explain this scenario consider a home automation system in customer needs to interact with digital switch board. Application generates events and there status is logged into file for later references if required. Now to perform operations related to file system need OS services. OS will have certain headers and built-in tools provided by C++ language. We need input stream to read file content into application and output stream to write application content to file. There are some standard tools that allows reading from keyboard and writing each key press in to file for further operations on file. These streams are called input stream and output stream respectively. Input stream feeds file content to application and output stream feeds application content to file for further use.

Following figures indicate file stream operation with respect to application and file on storage medium.

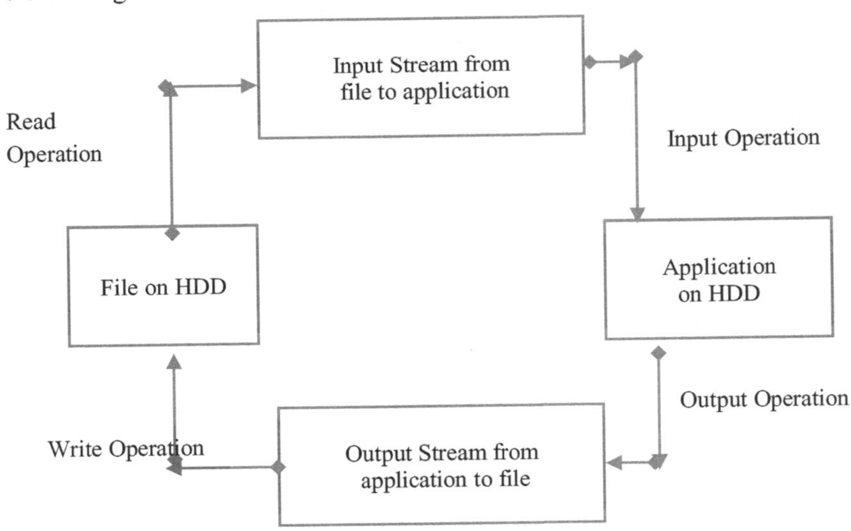

24.2 File Stream Operators

In C++ two operators are deals with input and output operation between application and console utility. They are input stream (>>) operator, information moves between console file to application utility. Information is feed to application since called input stream. Another is output stream (<<) operator, information moves between application utility to console file. Information is moves out of application is called output stream. Input and output streams are defined with respect to application utility i.e. coming in and moving out w.r.t. application keeping at centre.

Example:

```
cin >> variable-name; //input stream operation
cout << variable-name;    //output stream operation
```

24.3 File Handling Classes

In C++ some services are required from OS that is used by stream operators. Stream is a sequence of bytes are called binary streams. Now to take advantages of OS services and reduce the cost of coding each functionality there are built-in classes are available that are connected with OS services.

Below it is maintained files handling related classes in hierarchical form. Following figure represent hierarchical model of built-in support provided by C++ classes related to IO subsystems.

The base class is IOS called input output system. IOS class is inherited by two subsystem of class called console or terminal IO related classes and another is file that is disk related IO classes. Console related classes are "istream" looks at input related operations only and "ostream" looks at output related operations only. "iostream" class is inherited from "istream" and "ostream" gives combined operation related to console file. Disk related IO subsystem are called file handling related IO with respect to storage system. These classes are "ifstream" and "ofstream" are inherited from "fstreambase" class. Together classes gives operation related file reading, editing and writing changes to file. "ifstream" looks at input operations and "ofstream" looks at output operation with respect to electronic file storage on disk.

Figure below shows heirarchical organization of different file handling and IO related classes used and given for application writing.

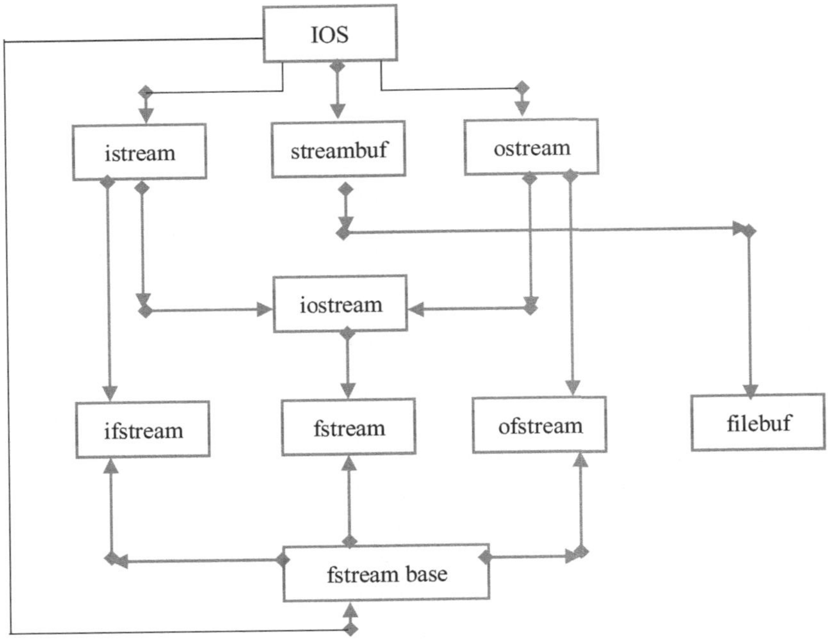

24.4 File Handling Classes and Its Use

File Handling Classes	File Handing API / Classes Explained
ifstream class	ifstream class is inherited from fstreambase class and provides built-in APIs for file handling related work. It provides following options to perform operation on file. Example, open () as a default mode, read(), seekg(), tellg(), getline(), get()
ofstream class	ofstream class is inherited from fstreambase class and provides built-in APIs for file handling related work. It provides following options to perform operation on file. Example, open () as a default mode, put(), seekp(), tellp(), write()
fstream class	fstream class inherits all the function from there base class istream and ostream via iostream class. Its default operation to work with file is through open() call. This class provides common operation related to disk IO.

filebuf class	Act as a common buffer requirement via filebuf during IO operations. Contains API close and open related to buffer operations
fstreambase class	Provides base class for fstream, ofstream, istream classes.

24.5 File Operation Modes

Application can open in three different modes as specified in file application. There are three mode of operations basically they are file read operation, file write operation and finally file edit mode operation. In read operation content of file is loaded from storage medium to application memory space. In write operation content of file from memory is stored into storage medium by creating a file on medium i.e. HDD, SD card etc. To explain this scenario consider a home automation system in customer needs to interact with digital switch board. To monitor user interaction with different options or fault detection programer needs to watch customer activity through local or remote logging on server machine called cloud logging. In such a case only we need output operation from application memory to storage media by creating a logger file. It uses only output stream. In case of configuration file such as XML files are used where needs only input stream only as strict requirement by client. To avail only unidirectional communication File Operation Modes are defined by application language like HLL (High Level Language).

Syntax:

```
file-handling-class-object.open(“FileName”, file-mode-of-
                    operation);
```

Example:

```
fstream mfStream (“WashingMachineLogging.log”,
                    ios::out);

fstream mfStream (“WashingMachineConfig.conf”, ios::in);
```

In example WashingMachineLogging.log file is created and it only purpose is to send information to storage media as mentioned above discussion. Logs events on Home Automation System into log file. Developer does only output operation from app memory to storage media.

File Operations Mode	Mode Explanation
ios :: app	Add content to end of existing file
ios :: ate	This moves file pointer to end of file
ios :: binary	Creates binary file
ios :: out	Opens file for writing only. No input operation is possible on respected file-name mentioned.
ios :: in	Opens file for reading only. No output operation is possible on respected file-name mentioned.
ios :: trunk	Delete content of old file and insert new content.
ios :: noreplace	File must not exist before IO operation performed on file. Open fails if file does exist prior.
ios :: nocreate	File must exist before IO operation performed on file. Open fails if file does not exist prior.

24.6 Opening and Closing of File

There are two approaches where file can be open by using constructor or by using open() method function call on represented object. Closing of a file stream on specified object is achieved by close() method function call on represented object.

Syntax:

```
ofstream mOFStream ("Filename");        //method-1
mOFStream.open("Filename");             //method-2
mOFStream.close(); // closing file stream already open file
in method-1 or method-2
```

24.7 Detecting End Of File (EOF)

To detect end pf file and to prevent further addition to "WashingMachineLogging.log" file, file end must be detected and appropriate action to be taken i.e. file byte stream to be closed by detection of EOF condition. To achieve proper operation w.r.t. file end "eof()" function allows developer to detect this condition. eof() is a member of IOS class and return non-zero value otherwise zero on reaching end of file condition.

Example:

```
ifstream mifStream ("WashingMachineLogging.log");
```

```
if( mifStream.eof() != 0) {
  mifStream.close();
            // Once pointer reaches EOF file must be closed to
avoid erroneous
}
// situation like corruption of file on abrupt exit of application
```

24.8 File Manipulators Pointers

Many times it required that to perform operation or insert a record at specific column and row. File manipulators pointer are achieve with manipulator API available in file stream classes in C++. Following table specifies built-in API related to file handling.

File Manipulators Pointer APIs	File Manipulator Explanation
ios :: beg	Moves file pointer to the beginning of file
ios :: cur	Gives current position of file pointer
ios :: end	Moves file pointer to the end of file
seekg(offset)	Moves file pointer from the beginning of file specified offset bytes
seekg(offset, position)	Moves file pointer from the offset of file specified offset positional bytes
tellg()	Gives current position of file pointer from beginning of file
seekp(offset)	Moves put pointer offset location forward from beginning w.r.t. output operation of file
seekp(offset, position)	Moves file pointer from the offset of file specified offset positional bytes w.r.t. output file operation
tellp()	Gives current position of file put pointer w.r.t. output operation of file

About File Manipulators Pointers:

Usually this file pointers are helpful in seeking intermediate position in file that are helpful in reading and writing file. One example I want to suggest you is to opening input file and writing it to another file of specific size. This kind of operation is required in case of video and text logging files where large logging of information into single file is not desirable. Suppose in operation theatre doctors surgery is recorded and wants to store in a single file. In this scenario if storage disk size gets full then its an complete loss of information so saving partial file into same disk is a significant step. Suppose your application is logger into text file then reading logger file of big size is a problematic approach as we seen in case of video files. Suppose I need a logging of crash issue in specific module at client side then i will go with whats happen in that specific module and not in case of entire dump created during crash since ts related to specific module.

A good example is to split files and streams coming from camera recording and disk recording into specific file size. One difficulty implementing single file is to empty disk space filled due to large logging it may be video logic of CCTV or any individual application logging that occupies large disk space as a single file. Now if such logging is required and occupies disk space in large its application developer is to keep required logging info and free up old files. Now to implant this one large file needs to be split into multiple files. This is advantages to free up disk space for other application and maintains need space for further use by freeing old logger files.

Algorithm:

Step1. Check input file exists;

Step2. If input file exists then open in read mode only.

Step3. Read input file in buffer.

Step4. Write to output file buffer in append mode.

Step5. Check output file size by using tellp() pointer. it gives file size in bytes.

Step6. After writing required bytes close input and output file pointers. Flush out output buffer. Break reading and writing loop.

Step7. Stop execution.

Example: In this example some help is taken from Qt library. You can ignore those and rewrite example in C++. it works fine.

```
#include <QCoreApplication>

#include <iostream>

#include <fstream>

#include <QDebug>
```

```
#include <QFile>
using namespace std;
int main(int argc, char *argv[])  {
   QCoreApplication a(argc, argv);
   ifstream *inputFile =  new ifstream;
   ofstream *outputFile  = new ofstream;
   char *ioFileData = new char[1024];
   unsigned int size = (1024 * 1024);
   QFile isInputFilExist;
   if(isInputFilExist.exists("01LET'SPARTY.mp3")==true) {
      qDebug()<<"File Exist";
      inputFile->open("01LET'SPARTY.mp3");
      qDebug()<<"File Opened";
      outputFile->open("01LET'SPARTYCopy.mp3",ios::app |
                                                   ios::binary);
      while(1) {
       inputFile->read(ioFileData,sizeof(ioFileData));
       outputFile->write(ioFileData,sizeof(ioFileData));
       unsigned int tellpOutputFilePtrSize = int (outputFile->tellp());
       qDebug()<<"OutputfileSize = "<<tellpOutputFilePtrSize;
        if(tellpOutputFilePtrSize > (size)) {
            qDebug()<<"File Written Sucessfully";
            inputFile->close();
            outputFile->close();
            outputFile->flush();
            qDebug()<<"File Streams Closed.";
            break;
        }
```

```
        }
    }
    return a.exec();
}
```

Output:

Original audio file is spliced into two separate file.

24.9 Inserting Object Info

In C++ information moves in form of runtime entities that is in abstracted and encapsulated form. Information is not allow to move freely with process. Many time its required to read in the object of class format. One such a example is database files. Employment related application written in C++ encapsulate individual record in object format and insert into database kind of filesystem. Application pushes object into database. Database file is enough intelligent identify and extract individual info inserting in database at proper place.

Syntax:

1. Inserting object into file i.e writing to file

```
fstream mfStmEmployeeInfo;
// create file stream object, initialise it and perform
// operation by step mentioned below
mfStmEmployeeInfo.write((char *) & object-name,
                        sizeof(object-name));
```

2. Reading information from file to application

```
mfStmEmployeeInfo.read((char *) & object-name,
                       sizeof(object-name));
```

Example:

```
#include <iostream>
#include <fstream>
#include <string>
using namespace std;
class ObjectToFileInfo {
```

```
        string mStrHouseName;
        int mIHouseNumber;
public:
        ObjectToFileInfo() :
        mStrHouseName(""),mIHouseNumber(0) {
        }
        void setHouseNumber(int lIHouseNumber) {
        mIHouseNumber = lIHouseNumber;
        }
        void setHouseName(string lStrHouseName) {
        mStrHouseName = lStrHouseName;
        }
        void displayHouseInfo() {
        cout<<"House Name : "<<mStrHouseName<<"\n";
        cout<<"House Number : "<<mIHouseNumber<<"\n";
        }
};
int main() {
        ObjectToFileInfo mMyHouseInfo;
        // Initialise Housing related info
        mMyHouseInfo.setHouseName("Shetye Girish Ajit H.");
        mMyHouseInfo.setHouseNumber(0107);

        fstream mMyHouseFile;
        mMyHouseFile.open("HouseOwnerFile.hsu",ios::out);
        // writing object into file
        mMyHouseFile.write((char *) & mMyHouseInfo,
                sizeof(mMyHouseInfo));
        mMyHouseFile.seekg(0);
```

```
        // moving pointer to begging of file
        mMyHouseFile.close();
        // closing file after write operation
        ObjectToFileInfo mMyHouseInfoTemp;
        // created temp object
        mMyHouseFile.open("HouseOwnerFile.hsu",ios::in);
        //opening to read file
        mMyHouseFile.read((char *) & mMyHouseInfoTemp,
                sizeof(mMyHouseInfoTemp));
        mMyHouseFile.seekg(0);
        mMyHouseFile.close();
        mMyHouseInfoTemp.displayHouseInfo();
        // display file through temp object
        return 0;
}
```

24.10 Summary

- In this chapter, we learn about reading/writing/updating and removing information to file on a disc.
- To perform operations on file we need file pointer. To avail file handler we need to include <fstream> header file in your source file. We can perform I/O operations on file.
- End of file is detected by special function "eof()". Once end of file is encountered, developer can perform closed operation on file.
- There are two pointers are available called seekg() and seekp(), and tellg() and tellp(). They specifies position of file pointer in file.

24.11 Hausaufgaben

Carefully study examples given in this chapter as they are of more importance and practically used in development environment.

Chapter 25.
I/O Manipulators

I/O manipulators are supported by C++ and language similar to OOPs concept. In C++ information is moved in stream format. These streams are either unformatted or formatted streams. Usually in lab we practice C++ using unformatted way. But in general many application required user-interface and formatted output to be delivered to client. C++ support both streams. Streams are normally called as byte stream since manipulation work is made on byte stream may be formatted or unformatted. Operator cout “<<“ are used for formatted output and called output stream and cin “>>” are used for formatted input stream to read record from particular file and shown on console. Operator cin (>>) and cout (<<) are used for console I/O formatted and unformatted operations. To explain this scenario consider a home automation system in customer needs to interact with digital switch board to monitor or to see monthly consumption of electric units connected. The bill to be generated on consumption of each unit. Billing information needs to in specific and ordered structure/format. To specify formatted information on bill generated by Home automation system need to give electricity board for payment plan. At customer end bill gets generated on e-bill by specifying individual details for each customer. E-Bill should contains current units, previous units, unit rates, company of distribution, consumer number, month of bill, discount offered and so on. Billing information is specified in particular format by saying width and height and maximum required space and to fill specific spaces with particular format specifiers manipulators are used. With formatted information with help of manipulator is given to printer to generate hard copy of electric unit consume by home automation system.

Organization and collection of printing information on digital or with printer in specific formatting layout is made available with manipulator in C++. Basically manipulators are used to show information in tabulated manner by specifying number of digit, index, height, width and then filling pattern, number of spaces to be left and so on, are implemented by manipulators of C++ and similar OOPs languages.

Another and much clear example of D-Mart Billing counters. After shopping at D-Mart customer comes to billing counter. At billing counter he/she shows all product purchase. Representative at billing counter generates bill. After payment billing information is given to printer to print bill and get clearance. Now, billing info is organized in specific format and layout to fit as per attached printer in specific way. To have organization and to have tabular organization of various filed of billing activity are made with the help of manipulators in C++. This is called formatted I/O in C++. Unformatted I/O does organize information in random format or unstructured way.

Types Of I/O Manipulators

1. Unformatted I/O Manipulators
2. Formatted I/O Manipulators

I/O manipulators are special functions that deals with I/O streams that changes how information to be shown in specific format or certain ways on digital platform. But it doesn't mean that programmer or developer changes or modifies information shown with the help of manipulators helping functions.

25.1 Unformatted I/O Manipulators

Unformatted I/O manipulators are operated with I/O operators as input (>>) and output (<<). There are special words are reserve for unformatted manipulators. They are also called as manipulators with no parameters. They are sole words that are used with I/O operators. They are defined in iostream library of C++.

flush: This operator forcefully flushes characters present in output stream to output device like console or in some file mentioned to have practical data such as logger file of home automation system. “flush” is available in ostream class in C++. To flush last line of logger file used in home automation system.

endl: This operator is called line-feed operator. It insert new line by ending current line and with inserting “\n” new line character at the end of present line and character pointer goes to beginning of next line. It also flushes output stream to console or file the same way as flush manipulator. To insert or to show new logs on next line in logger application.

ws: It is called whitespace i/o manipulator. It removes all whitespace present in specified in present string. “ws” is available in istrteam class in C++. To collect information for remote logging on server say cloud logging need to remove spaces present in string generated from local system.

ends: This is another I/O manipulator available in ostream class. it is used to insert null character at the end of string associated with output buffer. Sometimes need to restore logger file content into character array and to be process so that stored in cloud computing databases.

25.2 Formatted I/O Manipulators

Formatted I/O manipulators are special functions that insert formatted effect into C++ stream. These are available in "<iomanip>" header file in C++.

Formatted I/O Manipulators	Formatted I/O Manipulators Explanation
setw (int width)	It is used to set width of output to width value
setfill (int fill)	It is used to set fill character of output to fill value
setbase (int base)	It is used to set base of output to base value
setprecision (int pVal)	It is used to set precision value of output to pVal float value
resetiosflags (long flag)	It reset ios flag set by flag value
setiosflag (long flag)	It set ios flag set by flag value.
std::showbase	It indicates base of specified numeric value
std::noshowbase	It indicates no base of specified numeric value
std::boolalpha	It indicates true or false of specified boolean variable into true or false string value
std::noboolalpha	It indicates true or false of specified boolean variable into 1 or 0 value
std::showpoint	It shows point in floating values
std::noshowpoint	It doesn't show point in values except non zero flowing values
std::showpos	It shows + sign in-front of positive integers
std::noshowpos	It does not shows + sign in-front of positive integers but shows - sign.
std::skipws	It skips white space before any non whitespace character is found
std::noskipws	It doesn't skips white space before any non whitespace character is found.
std::uppercase	It forces uppercase values to ASCII characters.
std::nouppercase	It doesn't forces uppercase values to ASCII characters.
std::internal	It adjust field adding to set fill value to adjusted value
std::left	It adjust field to left
std::right	It adjust field to right

std::dec	It set decimal values that is base 10
std::hex	It set hexadecimal value that is base 16
std::oct	It set octal values that is base 8
std::fixed	It uses fixed decimal value
std::scientific	It uses scientific floating point notations to values

Example: In following example G.S.T. is displayed in formatted manner.

```
#include<iostream>
#include<iomanip>
using namespace std;
int main() {
        float showGSTOnBill = 1.1800;
        cout<<"G.S.T. On Bill = “<<showGSTOnBill<<endl;
                                        //output before formatting
        cout<<showpoint;                // manipulators
        cout<<showpos;
        cout<<setprecision(5);
        cout<<setfill('#');
        cout<<setw(20);
        cout<<right;
        cout<<"G.S.T. On Bill = "<<showGSTOnBill<<endl;
                                        //output after formatting
        return 0;
}
```

Output:

G.S.T. On Bill = 1.18

###G.S.T. On Bill = +1.1800

25.3 Summary

- In this chapter we learn about manipulators that they are used to format output i.e. a application developer present output data as they want in specific format. Example is information on printed receipt.
- To use manipulators developer needs to include “<iomanip>” header file into the application.
- There are formatted and unformatted I/O manipulators to deal with input and output information.

25.4 Hausaufgaben

- Write a application to read and write hotel billing info to be presented as on physical copy of bill.

  Example:

```
|_____  HOTEL PANCHTARA _____|
| Sr. no |__Menu Purchase__|__Price__|
|   1.   | Veg. Kolliwada  |  200    |
|   2.   | Veg. pulav      |  200    |
|   3.   | Masala Papad    |  70     |
|______|_________________|_______|
|_Total_|____3_Items______|__470___|
```

All components should have fixed width and right alignment for menu purchased, price to be center and amount to be right justified.

NOTES

Chapter 26

Namespaces and Scope Resolution in C++

In C++ project, when many files and classes, variables, functions are involved, it is great chance that developer use same variable name class name function name to describe a particular functionality in code. As it is obvious that programmer have less choice of using altogether different names for specific programming problems to solve. As code increases complexity overcomes developer skills. Developer starts creating code fix issue and waste development time. Time is most crucial factor in development of application. It cost money to a development client. It also increases and move focus on loss of revenue and cost to individual developer.

To address this issue C++ provides a concept called namespace in C++. With this, ambiguity in having same variable names, class names, function names are resolved to a great extent. One thing is once complicity increases then it is necessary to break coding into different visibility spaces by defying namespaces of tokens, keywords and variables. Even we use this concept, it is mandatory to have namespaces to be appropriately define to come to correct logical solutions. Mainly namespaces create issues when one class is defined or required by another class which required forward declaration of one class over another class thats come across different modules and use of libraries.

26.1 Scope Resolution (: :) Operator

Similar to above discussion about namespaces scope resolution (: :) operators are used to access global version of variable if redefine in inner block having same variable name. It always pointed to global version in local scope if redefine again.

Syntax:

```
::variable-name;

// access global value of variable in inner block if redefine   same
variable
```

Example:

```
#include <iostream>
using namespace std;
int bookPages = 200;
// global variable access using scope resolution (::) operator
int main() {
        int bookPages = 100; {
                int currentPages = 30;
                int bookPages    = currentPages;
                cout<<"Inner Block : "<<"\n";
                cout<<"Current Pages = "<<currentPages<<"\n";
                cout<<"Book Pages = "<<bookPages<<"\n";
                cout<<"Global Book Pages = "
<<::bookPages<<"\n";
        }
        cout<<"OuterBlock : "<<"\n";
        cout<<"Outer Book Pages = "<<bookPages<<"\n";
        cout<<"Global Book Pages = "<<::bookPages<<"\n";
}
```

Output:

```
        Inner Block :
        Current Pages = 30
        Book Pages = 30
        Global Book Pages = 200
        OuterBlock :
        Outer Book Pages = 100
        Global Book Pages = 200
```

26.2 Using Namespace

In above example we declared local namespace within main function called unnamed namespace. In this global variable is access by using scope resolution operator where no namespace scope is defined. As we already discuss use of namespace in application development project here we see specific example how to write namespace and access them using scope resolution (::) operator.

Syntax:

Defining namespace with keyword “namespace” followed by namespace-name.

```
namespace namespace-Name {
        body-of-namespace;
        // it may contain nested namespace, classes,
    functions, global variables etc.
}
```

Calling or allocating defined namespace using below syntax.

```
using namespace name_space;      or
using namespace::variable_In_Namespace;
```

This keyword is used to resolve naming convention whenmismatch happen for user specified variables or built-in type variables.

Example:

In this LED class is defined common but separated by namespaces since we can not use common name in same scope of class. It gives compiler error if occurred. In this UI is global namespace and BedRoom and Hall are namespace specific to LED class. There are two different methods are define which does turning on of respective room lights.

```
#include <iostream>
using namespace std;
namespace UI {
    namespace HomeAutomation {
            namespace Lights {
            namespace BedRoom {
```

```
            class LED {
                    int mOnAllLights;
        public:
            void onAllLightsOfBedRoom(int lOnAllLights) {
            cout<<"All bights Are Turn On Of Bed Room : " <<
                                        lOnAllLights <<"\n";
                    }
                }; //class LED ends here
            }
namespace Hall {
        class LED {
                    int mOnAllLights;
        public:
            void onAllLightsOfHall(int lOnAllLights) {
            cout<<"All lights Are Turn On of Hall : " <<
                                        lOnAllLights<<"\n";
                    }
            };
} } // namespace  ends here
} } // namespace ends here UI
using namespace UI::HomeAutomation::Lights;     //namespace declared
using namespace UI::HomeAutomation::Lights::BedRoom; //namespace
declared
int main() {
        LED bedRoom;
        bedRoom.onAllLightsOfBedRoom(2);
        Hall::LED hall;
        hall.onAllLightsOfHall(4);
```

```
        return 0;
}
```

Output:

```
        All lights Are Turn On Of Bed Room : 2
        All lights Are Turn On of Hall : 4
```

26.3 Type Cast (static/dynamic/reinterpret/const) _cast

In C++11 Following features are added to promote one type to another type that it may upcast or down cast to fundamental type.

26.3.1 static_cast

This keyword is used to convert or type cast from one type to another type of primitive type variables.

Example:

```
        float amtToPay = 1.5;
    int netAmtToPay = static_cast<int>(amtToPay);
  O/P = netAmtToPay = 1;
```

26.3.2 dynamic_cast

This keyword is used to convert or type cast from one type to another type of user-define type variables say object of classes. This mainly casting from base class to derived class. This technique is helpful in calling derived procedure/methods using base class object.

Example:

Convert Derived Class to its Base Class and invoke derived class if polymorphic.

```
    baseClassObj = dynamic_cast<Base*>(derivedClassObj)
class LEDs {
public:
        void onLEDS() {
        cout<<"LEDs are turned on"<<endl;
        }
```

```
};
class RegulatorLEDs {
public:
        void virtual onRegulatorLEDS() {
        cout<<"Regulator LEDs are turned on"<<endl;
        }
};
class HomeAutomation : public LEDs, public RegulatorLEDs {
public:
        void onHomeAutoRegulatorLEDS() {
        cout<<"Regulator LEDs are turned on"<<endl;
        }
        void onRegulatorLEDS() {
        cout<<"Home Automation of Regulator,LEDs are turned
                                        on"<<endl;
        }
};
int main() {
        LEDs *swicthOn = new LEDs;
        //RegulatorLEDs *regSwicthOn = dynamic_cast
        //<RegulatorLEDs*>(swicthOn);
        //This line of casting gives error since LEDs class is not
        //polymorphic.
        HomeAutomation *homeAuto = new HomeAutomation;
        RegulatorLEDs *regSwicthOn = dynamic_cast
                <RegulatorLEDs*>(homeAuto);
        regSwicthOn->onRegulatorLEDS();
        return 0;
}
```

Output:

Home Automation of Regulator,LEDs are turned on

26.3.3 reinterpret_cast

This keyword is used to convert or type cast from one type to another type of primitive type variables to pointer type and vice-versa.

pointer-variable = reinterpret_cast<ptr-datatype>(variable-name)

Example:

In this example two classes are independent but still through reinterpret_cast we are converting one pointer type to another pointer type and calling public methods of a class. Since no inheritance ship can be required and cast operation is successful.

```
class LEDs {
public:
        void onLEDS() {
        cout<<"LEDs are turned on"<<endl;
        }
};
class RegulatorLEDs {
public:
        void onRegulatorLEDS() {
        cout<<"Regulator LEDs are turned on"<<endl;
        }
};
int main() {
        LEDs *swicthOn = new LEDs;
        RegulatorLEDs *regSwicthOn= reinterpret_cast <
              RegulatorLEDs*>(swicthOn);
        regSwicthOn->onRegulatorLEDS();
        return 0;
```

```
}
```

Output:

Regulator LEDs are turned on.

26.3.4 const_cast

This keyword is used to override constant ness or volatileness.

```
#include<iostream>
using namespace std;
int main() {
        const int lID = 110011;
        const int *mID = &lID;
cout<<"Before Change In Constant-ness  = "<<*mID<<endl;
        int *iD = const_cast<int*>(mID);
        *iD = 5000;        //after change in constant-ness
cout<<"After Change In Constant-ness= “<<(*mID)<<endl;
cout<<"Original Value, Since Constant-ness Removed = “<<        lID <<endl;
        return 0;
}
```

Output:

Before Change In Constantness = 110011

After Change In Constantness= 5000

Original Value Since Constantness Removed = 110011

26.4 mutable Keyword

Consider a sitruation where we have transcation id and reference transcation id. Now on successful transcation say banking there is no need to update both ids as they are correct on transcation. So no worries. But in case of failure of transcation, transcationId remains the same but we need to update reference transcation id to new id i.e. referenceTranscationId. Say online booking of movie ticket fails.

So this phenomena is observed with when we have const object created finally that doesnot allow to change data inside it because of its constantness. "mutable" kehyword is help us to update reference transcation id and not the unique transcation id. Mutable keyword works without removing constantness and or without casting object by const_cast. Other way to do this is to remove constantness by using const_cast operator as stated in above topic.

Syntax:

```
mutable int refId;
```

Example:

```
class ConstMutableObject {
public:
   const int id;
   mutable int refId;
   ConstMutableObject (int lId,int lRefId) :
                                    id(lId),refId(lRefId) {
   showId();
   }
   void showId();
};
void ConstMutableObject :: showId() {
   cout<<"ID = "<<id<<endl;
   cout<<"Refernce ID = "<<refId<<endl;
}
int main() {
 const ConstMutableObject mu(1001,2002);
//comment below line and run the code
 mu.id = 3003;  // this statement gives error while we re-assign id     // variable
from 1001 to new value 3003.
mu.refId = 5005; // this statement doesnt give error as we craeted of //   mutable
type. We can override its constantness.
```

```
cout<<" Refernce ID = "<<mu.refId<<endl;  //refId updated to new value
return 0;
}
```

Output:

ID = 1001

Refernce ID = 2002

Refernce ID = 5005 //updated one because of mutable

Refer following table for topic mentioned and its explanation.

Typeid	This keyword is used to extract type info of a primitive and user-defined type object in type_info datatype. It requires <typeinfo> header file.
using	This keyword is used to apply namespace for particular type when conflict occurs. using namespace Hall;
wchar_t	This keyword is used to specify character of 2byte long as usually char is one byte long. wchar ch = L'G'
Typename	This keyword is used to define type name of variables and not its type.

Convert byte into float value.

Compare int and hex can it gives same result without conversion.

Topic Covered in Part III

C++ Language Specifications

Chapter 27.

Introduction to Advance Features in C++

27.1 Introduction

After specifying new standards for C language by Bjarne Stroustrup, in 1983 C language become C++ language. They added lots of new features satisfying programming or development requirement and developer requirement too. In C, data moves openly around system called functional programing become OOPs (Object Oriented Programming) parody. In C++ data moving round system become part and bounded by OOPs principles. In this object-oriented programming introduce to software development world. Many issues in functional programming will be handled by C++ by using OOPs principles. Software development becomes comparatively easy. Information wrapped in by OOPs concept.

After introduction of oops, in later revision to C++ as C++98 STL (Standard Template Library) was introduce. In this concept generic programming is put forward. Same set of code is more generically used for solving development need. So different information or data start responding to not same but same set of code. Here different set of code for different set of information or data is generated by generic programming in C++. Information started on storing containers a generic type of class object where type need to be specified and code generation is handled by that language compiler i.e. C++ compiler say GCC by GNU (GNU C++ Compiler). These features introduce to have new functional requirement and to provide more language related tools or components to have most usable and become developer modern day choice for software writing.

With journey to become most preferable language, they introduce C++11 standards in August 2011 to C++ and C++ become more robust, more preferred, more usable, more flexible, less dependable on 3rd party tools, richer in features and more widely accepted language. The most prominent feature introduce is "threads". With introduction to threads language removes its dependency on "pthread" library based on Linux kernel. There are two ways to have processing information. One is you process it step by step one after another or perform simultaneous operation on data. This is called concurrent programming.

Concurrent threads execute by switching its context and giving chance to another thread in same process and on same CPU (Central Processing Unit). It gives intuition of multitasking and parallel programming. Another approach is to have parallel programming. In this to happen parallelism of execution of code is based on multiple hardware i.e. CPUs on that actual thread gets executed having parallel programing. Rather than having single CPU here we have multiple CPU for execution. For example, in high end computing DSP (Digital Signal Processor) and Math processors are attached with CPU to have parallel programing, so that in less CPU cycles more information is process. As faster comparatively to concurrent programming. These benefits C++ language on introduction of threads in C++11 standards. And these threads are native to C++ language APIs.

27.2 Features Of C++98/99

1. Addition of STL (Standard Template Library)
2. Addition of auto keyword

27.2.1 Addition of STL (Standard Template Library)

STL is a set of libraries designed by using feature of template programming or way to use template feature of C++. We called it as a generic programming. In this, generic class or function is created to manipulate information attached with class or function or both at a time. We can write our own class or function using template feature.

The Standard Template Library (STL) have some predefined classes and functions already built-in and as a part of C++ language. This STL libraries are designed for programmer, developer in ready to use form by designer Alexander Stepanov for C++ programming language based of template feature of C++. Stepanov introduces many classes as per proposed design by C++ committee and now these classes are part of C++ STL libraries. Some classes are vector, list, stack, map etc. and more you can refer google for additional information available over online media.

Since these classes are template based, additional processing power or say features are needed by language. Say to support STL, additionally four components are introduced and they are containers, algorithms, iterators and functions. Let's see these in brief.

1. Container.

Container as name suggest, it is used to container means to use to contain or hold inside it something. This something is nothing but a type of information, say it may be class type or build-in type or pointer type. When we create class or function it is very necessary to tell kind of information it holds. Now to hold information of specified type we need container class.

Now you have understood that container is class of specific type to hold information of that type inside it.

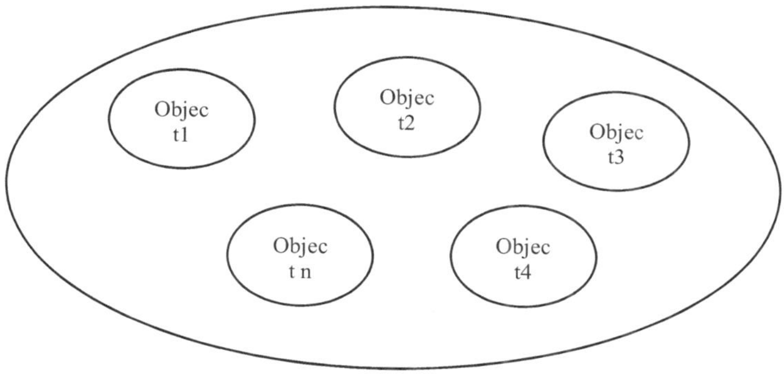

Container with its objects as information or data elements

Above figure represent container which can hold n objects inside it of specific type. This type must be specified at the creation of container say vector, list, stack or say map. In case of map, it becomes associative container of key value pair type. In container all the information is of same type. You cannot hold class of men and women in same container. This is only possible when you have common base class for both type of information. Say Humans is a base class for both men and women. So, container holds information of Humans type that represent both men and women.

Example is ticketing where men and women are serving as per their occurrences in line or say queue. Information in queue of generic type that represent both type of information says Humans.

Example: Ticketing System

```
        #include <vector>
        using namespace std;
class HumenTicketSystem {
public:
```

```
  HumenTicketSystem() {  }
};
class Men : public HumenTicketSystem {
public:
  Men () { }
  void calledMen() {
    cout<<"I am men, Give me men ticket"<<endl;
  }
};
class Women : public HumenTicketSystem {
public:
  Women () { }
  void calledWomen() {
    cout<<"I am women, Give me women ticket"<<endl;
  }
};
int main () {
  cout << "Created Container of Vector type!" << endl;
  vector<HumenTicketSystem*> ;
  ticketSystem.push_back(new Men());
  ticketSystem.push_back(new Women());
  Men *obj_men = (Men *) ticketSystem.at(0);
  obj_men->calledMen();
  Women *obj_women = (Women *) ticketSystem.at(1);
  obj_women->calledWomen();
  return 0;
}
```

Output:

Created Container of Vector type!

I am men, Give me men ticket

I am women, Give me women ticket

In the above example of ticketing system, there are two different type of information is held by vector class. Since possible because of common base type. Here vector class act as a container for men and women type. Since base type is of Humen, to resolve function call we must tell type that on which method is called. It is very necessary to cast general type into specific type. I use push_back() and at() api from vector class that simplifies my work of handling types.

There are container types as

1. Sequence Container

   Sequence container are classes of template type that used to store data element inside it. These data elements can be of different type stored. To perform operation on data or information element we need to have sequential access approach i.e. information is sequentially accessing form either end. This is depending on various algorithms supported by that container. Access elements sequentially by sequence container. As size of sequence container increases their time complexity increases and take time to perform operation on them. If any container contains one lakh elements or more, then its operational performance seriously gets affected.

   Example: vector, array, list etc.

2. Associative Container and Unordered Associative Container

   As we have seen Associative Container and Unordered Associative Containers are same as sequential container except in Associative container information is tied to particular key representing that information or data element. To access particular information set in a container developer needs to refer key associated with data elements. Information is stored in ordered fashion. In case of un-ordered Associative container data elements are stored in random ordered fashion. It is not necessary that element inserted will get inserted at 10th position or may get inserted at 5th position in container holding information. Rest is same for each container. As size of associative container increases their time complexity increases and take time to perform operation on them is same for each data element. If any container contains one lakh elements or more, then its operational performance remains same since key is unique for each container object.

Example: set, map, unordered map etc.

2. Algorithms

In above example, we have seen two APIs one is "push_back()" and another is "at()" are used to perform some operation on container class. They are called algorithms APIs specific to particular container here "vector". Further say algorithm is logical operation performed on information stored in particular object we say in the container. There are many algorithms attached to specific container class. Algorithms operate on objects in container class. To perform operation on containers object, a developer can define his own custom algorithm that is also possible.

Example: sort (), search () etc.

3. Iterators

In previous discussion we have seen containers and algorithms. Since we know container is a collection of homogeneous objects stored in containers memory. Here one issue is that container contains many data elements inside it. This container memory is available on heap. So, to travers on each data elements say objects we need some kind of pointers that points to each data element one after another. Now these pointers pointing to first element or in-between or last element. To hold pointers and to travers over containers elements we need iterators. These are special classes with algorithms that can be used to take each element from container and perform manipulation on each taken data elements. They are called iterators.

There are five different iterators and they are as below,

1. Input Iterator

   These iterators are used to read data elements from container.

2. Output Iterator

   These iterators are used to write into data elements from container.

3. Forward Iterator

These iterators are used to read, write and to move handle in forward direction. With these we can not move from reverse direction and we can not apply reverse search algorithm to them.

4. Bidirectional Iterator

   These iterators are same as forward iterators except we can perform reverse operation from last element of container to first element say by applying reverse search algorithm.

5. Random Access Iterators

   With this iterator we can apply bidirectional algorithm to selection of any data element in any order. Iterator can iterate any no of steps less than size in any one direction.

Example:

```
        #include <map>
        #include <string>
        #include <iterator>
        using namespace std;
class HumenTicketSystem {
public:
  HumenTicketSystem() { }
};
class Men : public HumenTicketSystem {
public:
  Men () {   }
  void calledMen() {
     cout<<"I am men, Give me men ticket"<<endl;
  }
};
class Women : public HumenTicketSystem {
public:
```

```
  Women () {    }
  void calledWomen() {
     cout<<"I am women, Give me women ticket"<<endl;
  }
};
int main () {
   cout << "Welcome to Iterators on Containers Elements" << endl;
   std::map<string,HumenTicketSystem*> ticketSystem;
   // here we used random access to store data elements
ticketSystem.insert(pair<string,HumenTicketSystem*>(string("Men"),        new
Men()));
ticketSystem.insert(pair<string,HumenTicketSystem*>(string("Women"),   new
Women()));
   // we will use iterators over map container to fetch tickets information
   map<string, HumenTicketSystem*> :: iterator map_itr;
   for  (map_itr   =   ticketSystem.begin();   map_itr   !=   ticketSystem.end();
++map_itr) {
      if(map_itr->first == string("Women")) {
         Women *women = (Women*) map_itr->second;
         women->calledWomen();
      }
   }
   return 0;
}
```

Output:

```
        Welcome to Iterators on Containers Elements
        I am women, Give me women ticket
```

In this example, we used map as a container and with that begin (), end () as an algorithm of map container. And finally, iterator of map type to travers over

container. In case of map, there are two pointers of iterator type are “first” that represent key in a map and “second” represent value associated with that key. Map stores data element in key value pair.

4. Functions

   Functions here called as a function pointer to element stored in container are invoked on data elements. They are called as functors. They mimic work of functions with argument and give call to container algorithms.

27.2.2 auto keyword

Keyword “auto” used to hold type that resulted from initialize expression. In C++98 auto variables have auto storage class with local lifecycle. This keyword is revisited and given additional meaning we see this under C++11 specification in up next discussion.

Example:

```
int a = 10;          auto b = a;

auto x = new HomeAutomation ();
```

Here, x will be of type HomeAutomation.

NOTES

Chapter 28
Algorithms in C++ STL

28.1 Introduction

In previous chapter we understand that algorithms are useful to perform logical operation on data elements inside container. The C++ Standard Template Library (STL) provides a rich set of algorithms that can be utilized to perform various operations on containers (such as arrays, vectors, etc.). These algorithms are accessible through the <algorithm> header. Depending on what type of operations performed by the algorithm, we categories them in some commonly used types. They are as below,

28.2 Sorting Algorithms.

As name said, sorting algorithms are used to sort or rearrange information in data elements or say objects in container. Following are many but here we name few examples of algorithms used sorting technique,

Uses Sort Technique	Explanation
sort ()	Sorts elements in a range
stable_sort ()	Sorts elements while preserving the order of equivalents
partial_sort ()	Partially sorts elements in a range.
partial_sort_copy ()	Copies and partially sorts a range
is_sorted ()	Checks whether a range is sorted

Example:

Refer google or ChatGPT for complex examples.

Searching Algorithms:

As name said, searching algorithms are used to search or find information in data elements or say objects in container. Following is many but here we name few examples of algorithms used searching technique,

Uses Search Technique	Explanation
find ()	Searches for a value in a range
binary_search ()	Determines if a value exists in a sorted range
lower_bound ()	Finds the first element not less than a given value
upper_bound ()	Copies and partially sorts a range

equal_range ()	Checks whether a range is sorted
count ()	Counts occurrences of a value in a range

Example:

Refer google or ChatGPT for complex examples.

28.3 Copying Algorithms:

As name said, copying algorithms are used to copy or move information in data elements or say objects in container either based on condition or direction. Following is many but here we name few examples of algorithms used searching technique,

Uses Copy Technique	Explanation
copy ()	Copies a range of elements
copy_if ()	Copies certain elements based on a condition
copy_backward ()	Copies a range of elements backward
move ()	Copies and partially sorts a range
swap_ranges ()	Exchanges values between two ranges

Example:

Refer google or ChatGPT for complex examples.

28.4 Counting Algorithms

As name said, counting algorithms are used to count occurrence of a value or count of information in data elements or say objects in container based on condition. Following are many but here we name few examples of algorithms used searching technique,

Uses Count Technique	Explanation
count ()	Counts occurrences of a value in a range
count_if ()	Returns the number of elements satisfying a condition
mismatch ()	Finds the first position where two ranges differ
equal ()	Tests whether elements in two ranges are equal
is_permutation ()	Checks if a range is a permutation of another

Example:

Refer google or ChatGPT for complex examples.

Chapter 29
Advance Features in C++11 Standards

29.1 Introduction

First of we need to understand that why in C++, a OOPs based language need revision in its own language. In 2011, hardware market and existing software market product start with many new features to adjust with complex customer requirements. Java is leading with many products in market. But the problem with such a language is that it suits specific or configured hardware and software. So, moving to new product needs specific configuration supported by language. Portability is a problem facing many products in market. Platform dependency is a major challenge and cost high for many product companies.

To mitigate with those issues a language with many new implementation features is required in embedded industry. To overcome software implementation complexities with minimum code and maximum coding results that is optimize coding are industry requirement. A language that is closed to hardware and software is identified by industry experts and that is by choice is C and C++. Many new features are introduced in C++ since 2011 and still going on ahead. C++11 is a major revision introduce in C++ since 2011.

29.2 Features Introduce in C++11 specification

Below list contains features introduce in C++ in 2011 becomes C++11 standards as below,

1. auto
2. nullptr
3. shared_ptr
4. strongly typed Enums
5. static_assert
6. variadic template
7. range based for loop
8. Initializer list

9. noexcept

10. move constructor and assignment operator

11. lambda expression

12. default and deleted member function

13. override identifier

14. threads

15. unordered containers 16. tuple

29.2.1 auto keyword

Before starting discussion on "auto" keyword, something term we use is inference. What its mean is that is to evaluate expression and give its result based on evaluation. In evaluation process, output is depending on expression. This will vary in each case. Developer doesn't know until expression is evaluated at execution. In such a scenario to determine type of final expression evaluation will be marked as auto. Keyword auto holds final type after expression evaluation.

Syntax:

```
auto variable_name = (expression);
```

Example:

```
for (auto map_itr = ticketSystem.begin();
        map_itr != ticketSystem.end (); ++map_itr) {
/*
    In this for loop type of variable map_itr is determine at
  compile time and we can correct any issue comes with
  expression evaluation and fixed before code crashes because of
violation in expression.
*/
Perform operation through variable whose type is determine via "auto"
keyword.
}
```

Keyword auto is very helpful in case of iterators and template type expressions where compiler replaces generic code with its type specified.

29.2.2 Keyword nullptr

In C++11, the keyword nullptr is used to replace or not to say replace but use instead of it. The problem with NULL macro used to determine null-ness of allocated memory is quite confusing with by saying equals to "0" i.e. zero. This is problematic when we compare with integer expression saying (i == 0) or (i == NULL). To mitigate or to avoid confusion and C++11 is more type specific, C++11 committee introduces new way to represent type check by using "nullptr" keyword.

Expression (i == NULL) or (i == 0) and (i == nullptr) are different.

Example:

```
int var = 100;

int *pointer = nullptr; // we used this in C++ to check null ness of
            //pointer type

if (pointer == nullptr) {

        pointer = new int;          // allocate memory

        pointer = &var;

} else {

    pointer = &var; //perform operation on allocated memory

}


cout<<" Value In pointer ==  "<<(* pointer);
```

Output:

Value In pointer == 100.

29.2.3 Template Class shared_ptr

In C++11, committee introduces smart pointers. What they basically do is to control the life cycle of pointer variable as specially of class type. It controls allocation of memory and its deallocation on heap specifically or allocated by new operator and deleted by delete keyword. Call to particular constructor and destructor is controlled by these smart pointers. In smart pointers, shared pointer is one example. In shared pointer uses a technique class resource counter. It is a variable that monitors how many times memory chunk is allocated. In below example is two times when (t_company = t_employee) is added to the code. See example 2. As you will find resource monitoring variable incremented to count 2. This count decremented on each destructor called but keep at least one chuck of memory until it goes to 0 and finally deletes last chunk when it becomes 0 i.e. zero. So, by reference counting on allocated memory, it decides to delete a final memory block avoiding memory leaks on particular resource.

Syntax:

```
shared_ptr < class_T > m_obj (arguments that matches class_T);
```

Example:

Refer class written before in chapter 19, declared as QCustomString as exactly same and then refer below main function call.

```
int main () {

shared_ptr <QCustomString > t_company(new
            QCustomString("Capgemini"));


cout<<"Company Name = "<<*t_company<<endl;

cout<<"Adress Pointed By t_company == "<< t_company.get()
                                   <<endl;

cout<<"Use Count = "<<t_company.use_count()<<endl;

{

    shared_ptr <QCustomString > t_employee(new
      QCustomString("Shetye Girish"));

      /* line no xyz:

         Add, ( t_company = t_employee) here

         Replace all instance of t_employee with t_comapny and      see
result.

      */

   cout<<"Employee Name = "<<*t_employee<<endl;

   cout<<"Adress Pointed By t_employee == "
                                    << t_employee.get() << endl;
```

```
        QCustomString employee = *t_company + " " + *t_employee;
        cout <<employee << endl;
        cout<<"Final Use Count = "<<t_employee.use_count()<<endl;
    }
  cout<<"Final Use Count after pointer = " <<
          t_company.use_count()   <<endl;
    return 0;
}
```

Output 1:

```
Company Name = Capgemini
Adress Pointed By t_company == 00000134B2E35BF0
Use Count = 1
Employee Name = Shetye Girish
Adress Pointed By t_employee == 00000134B2E361C0
Capgemini Shetye Girish
Final Use Count = 1
Destructor Called, Destructor Called
Final Use Count after pointer = 1, Destructor Called
```

Output 2:

```
(after adding line xyz and replace object to t_company within braces)
Company Name = Capgemini
Adress Pointed By t_company == 0000023DC36C39A0
Use Count = 1
Destructor Called
Employee Name = Shetye Girish
Adress Pointed By t_employee == 0000023DC36C3970
Shetye Girish
Final Use Count = 2
```

Destructor Called

Final Use Count after pointer = 1

Destructor Called

29.2.4 Strongly Typed Enums

In C++, enums are used to define constant or states required to or determine by application. This is same in C++11 and later versions. But major change is enums are strictly type in later implementation.

In previous discussion we seen some constants are define of enum type. Here also we define enums but they are strictly type. They are accessed by using its type. Basically, these enums are named constant for integers declared to give it a name.

Syntax:

```
enum class enum_type {
        LED_OFF = 0,
        LED_ON = 1
};
```

To access enums following syntax is used as below,

enum_type::LED_OFF or enum_type::LED_ON.

Example:

```
Enum class BedRoom {
        LED_OFF = 0,
        LED_ON = 1
};
```

To make state of home automation of lights application is as below,

BedRoom::LED_OFF or BebRoom::LED_ON instead of LED_OFF or LED_ON.

29.2.5 static_assert

static_assert keyword is used to generate compile time error messages rather crashing code at run time. It simplifies developer work before production. Before C++11 this is achieved using macro called "#error".

Syntax:

```
static_assert ( constant expression , "assert message" );
```

Example:

```
const int count = 10;

static_assert( count >= 10, "Count Should be more than or
        equla to 10.");
```

Assert message is evaluated only when constant expression is false otherwise no assertion on expression evaluation.

29.2.6 Variadic Template

Variadic templates are templatized function or class that take any number of arguments of different types. Those functions and classes that mimics this behavior are known as or called variadic templates function or class.

Variadic templates are very much useful in defining containers that holds different types of information. Say, as we previously discuss map as a container class. In that we hold information of primitive type or user-define type by saying template argument. If we write custom class with variadic template type then it is possible to hold variable information in that container.

With variadic template we can do generic programming with type-safe arguments. It is possible to have generic algorithm or data structure that operates on generic data. We can say that with template advantage developer can process information that is not specific to template type.

1. Variadic Template Function

Syntax:

```
template (typename T1, typename … Tany)

return_type function_name ( T1 arg1, Tany … arg2 ) {        …

return if any;
```

```
} //closed function body
```

Example:

```
template <typename Type1, typename ... Type2>
void showcards (Type1 value1, Type2 ... value2) {
cout<<"Value 1 = "<<value1<<endl;
((cout<<"Value 2 = "<<value2<<" "<<endl), ...);
}
int main () {
showcards ("Hearts", 10, "Diamond", 12, 13);
showcards ("Hearts", 10, "queen", 12, "king");
return 0;
}
```

2. Variadic Template Class

Variadic template class is a more generic way to define templates of variadic type. Based on type particular version of template class is used to generate code and its matching argument is called by checking type by compiler.

Syntax:

```
template <typename T, typename ... TArgs>
class ClassName {
//use template type as per your logic or convenience
};
```

Example:

```
template<typename T1, typename... T2> class Fruit;
template<typename T>
class Fruit<T> {
public:
T get () {
```

```
            return m_fruit_val;
                    }
                    void set (const T fruitVal) {
            m_fruit_val = fruitVal;
               }
            private:
               T m_fruit_val;
            };
template<typename T1, typename... T2>
class Fruit: public Fruit<T1>, public Fruit<T2 ...>
{
public:
   template<typename T>
   T Get () {
      return this->Fruit< T >:: get ();
   }
   template<typename T>
   void Set (const T fruitVal) {
      this->Fruit<T >:: set (fruitVal);
   }
};
int main (int args, char *[])
{
   Fruit<int, double, string> apple;
   apple.Set<int>(4);
   apple.Set<double>(23.99);
   apple.Set<std::string>("Apple Fruit");
```

```
    cout << "Fruit Size: "<< apple.Get<int>() <<endl;
    cout << "Fruit Price: "<< apple.Get<double>() <<endl;
    cout << "Fruit Name: "<< apple.Get<std::string>() <<endl;
    return 0;
}
```

29.2.7 Range based for loop

Range based for loop is more convenient and flexible way to traverse over container elements over traditional use of iterators. Iterators use index-based approach over element-based approach or item pushed in a container approach. The new way is very much easy to understand and more readable as convenient to visualize.

Syntax:

```
for (auto object: container_object) {
// process object that is taken from container.
// for loop will terminate on last element from container.
// or explicitly break on specific condition.
}
```

Example:

```
#include <iostream>
#include <vector>
#include <string>
using namespace std;
class ForLoop: public vector<string> {
    string m_names;
public:
    ForLoop ():m_names("") {
    }
    string getNames() const {
        return m_names;
```

```
    }
    void addNames() {
        push_back(m_names);
    }
    void popData() {
        pop_back();
    }
    void setNames(const string& names) {
        m_names = names;
    }
    void addNames(const string& names) {
        setNames(names);
        push_back(m_names);
    }
};
int main () {
    ForLoop loopObj;
    loopObj.setNames(string("Girish"));
    loopObj.addNames();
    loopObj.setNames(string("Ganesh"));
    loopObj.addNames();
    loopObj.addNames(string("Harish"));
    for (auto dataObj: loopObj) {
        cout<<"Names = "<<dataObj<<endl;
    }
return 0;
}
```

29.2.8 Initializer list

Initializer list and member initializer list of a class is completely different from what we are talking about initializer list. Initializer list is a class of template type that allows initialization of template type parameters. Using this class, we can directly initialize array type, vector type or any class type.

The main advantage of initializer list is to return multiple values encapsulated as single parameter. Only thing is that we need to tell type of parameters that it receives. Allocation of memory to this list is contagious. Once list is ready, we cannot change/modify its data. Those list parameters act as immutable values or read only information. Copied object and original object contains same elements. Following are member functions such as begin (), end (), size (), empty () and data () are having their usual meaning associated with list initializer.

Syntax:

```
#include <initializer_list> // ....... header file

initializer_list < T > list = { T1, T2, T3, ...., Tn };
```

Example:

```
initializer_list < int > returnInitializerList () {

    return {10, 20, 30, 40, 50, 60};

} // defined here
initializer_list < int > int_list = returnInitializerList ();
// called here
```

29.2.9 noexcept Operator

The idea behind is to introduce noexcept operator is to have type safe operation. Developer must know how to handle or what action to be taken on when type safe situation occurs in software design. So, once we know what to do, developer can use "noexpect" with function of class type or without that. An example I can give you is a home automation system where suddenly lights off and we have thrown exception to handle it that cause sudden switch off of electricity board as to take care of situation. But if we know to take corrective measure then throwing exception have no point and we can use safely “noexcept”.

Syntax:

noexpect (expression)   or

noexpect

Example:

```
// following example is from website www.learncpp.com
class Doomed {
public:
   ~Doomed () {
      cout << "Doomed destructed\n";
   }
};
void thrower () {
   cout << "Throwing exception\n";
   throw 1;
}
void pt () {
   cout << "pt (potentally throwing) called\n";
   Doomed doomed {};
   thrower ();
   cout << "This never prints\n";
}
void nt () noexcept {
   cout << "nt (noexcept) called\n";
   // This object will be destroyed during stack unwinding
   // (if it occurs)
```

```
    Doomed doomed {};
    thrower ();
    cout << "this never prints\n";
}
void tester (int c) noexcept {
    cout << "tester (noexcept) case " << c << " called\n";
    try {
        (c == 1)? pt (): nt ();
    }
    catch (...) {
        cout << "tester caught exception\n";
    }
}
int main () {
    cout << std::unitbuf; // flush buffer after each insertion
    cout << std::boolalpha; // print boolean as true/false
    tester (1);
    cout << "Test successful\n\n";
    tester (2);
    cout << "Test successful\n";
    return 0;
}
```

29.2.10 Exception safety guarantees

An exception safety guarantee is a contractual guideline about how functions or classes will behave in the event an exception occurs. There are four levels of exception safety guarantees:

No guarantee:

There are no guarantees about what will happen if an exception is thrown (e.g. a class may be left in an unusable state)

Basic guarantee:

If an exception is thrown, no memory will be leaked and the object is still usable, but the program may be left in a modified state.

Strong guarantee:

If an exception is thrown, no memory will be leaked and the program state will not be changed. This means the function must either completely succeed or have no side effects if it fails. This is easy if the failure happens before anything is modified in the first place, but can also be achieved by rolling back any changes so the program is returned to the pre-failure state.

No throw / No fail guarantee:

The function will always succeed (no-fail) or fail without throwing an exception (no-throw).

29.2.10 move constructor and assignment operator (=)

In C++11 move constructor and assignment operator are introduce to have better controlled over coping data from one object memory to another object of same type. The drawback of calling copy constructor and using assignment operator is that they invoke multiple times to copy data to same object and same memory location that may not require. This philosophy of copy data to same object leads to burden on application of repeated calls. This coping is done by l-value method and copy by move semantics is done by r-value method. Use of r-value method is more efficient than calling copy constructor with overloaded assignment operator.

Calling move constructor and overloading move assignment operator for copy information from one object memory to another object left memory in safe i.e. valid and keep object in unspecified state which is not invalid one.

Syntax:

```
        class MoveConstructor {
    public:
        MoveConstructor (MoveConstructor &&) {
        //this is move constructor
        //define your logic for move constructor
```

```
}
MoveConstrructor & operator = (MoveConstructor&& tempObj) {
return *this; //logic for copy object by r-value method.
}};
```

Example:

```
class MoveConstructor {
int* data;
public:
MoveConstructor(int info) : data (new int{info}) {
  //initialize data pointer to info
}
MoveConstructor (MoveConstructor&& mcobj) : data(mcobj.data) {
    mcobj.data = nullptr;
}
MoveConstructor& operator= (MoveConstructor&& otherMCObj) noexcept {
        if (this != &otherMCObj) {
          delete data;   //release current resource
          data = otherMCObj.data; //take ownership of other resources
          otherMCObj.data = nullptr; //release ownership
        }
  return *this;
  }
  void showData (std::string tstr) {
    cout<<"Object :  "<<tstr<<"\nData "<<(*data)<<endl;
    //re-run by commenting above cout statement
    //uncommnet below line and see output
    //cout<<"Object :  "<<tstr<<"\nData "<<(data)<<endl;
```

```
    }
};
int main () {

        MoveConstructor mc1 (10);
         mc1.showData("mc1"); //10
         MoveConstructor mc2 (100);
         mc2.showData("mc2"); //100
         MoveConstructor mc3 = std::move(mc1);
         mc3.showData("mc3"); //10
         mc3 = std::move(mc2);
         mc3.showData("mc3"); //100
         mc2.showData("mc2"); //0 see result after move operation

       return 0;
}
```

29.2.11 Lambda expression ()

Now before going to details into lambda expression first, we need to understand that it needs of use. Consider below example where function is called using callback technique i.e. with the help of callback pointer or say function pointer. The need is when we want to pass inline function or say function or rather say expression that validate condition and give its result. I want to say that in C++, we cannot pass if statement directly to any function from which I need result back. To achieve result from such an expression I need to define or take help of function pointers as shown in below example.

Example:

```
       void func_X (int x) {
 if (x > 5)
       cout<<x<<" is greater than 5"<<endl;
 else
```

```
        cout<<x<<" is less than or equal to 5"<<endl;
        }
    int main () {
      void (*callFunc_X) (int x) = &func_X;
    callFunc_X (100);
        return 0;
    }
```

In example above we need to define a function with name and then to use function pointer. Now alternative to above situation C+11 introduces lambda expressions. In this technique we don't need to write function rather we simply define anonymous function that does the job of evaluate expression where they define. No extra effort to write function pointers. With the added advantage of no need to write pointers. Lambda expression is effect in case of inline functions where less computations and quick results are expected. Lambda expression automatically deduce return type but in case of some complex expression we can explicitly specify return type.

Syntax:

```
auto variable = [capture](parameters) -> return_type {
                        // few statements …
                        }
```

You can capture by both reference and value, which you can specify using & and = respectively:

- [&obj_1, obj_2] captures obj_1 by reference and obj_2 by value
- [&] captures all variables used in the lambda by reference
- [=] captures all variables used in the lambda by value
- [&, obj_2] captures all variables used in the lambda by reference but captures obj_2 by value
- [=, &obj_1] captures all variables used in the lambda by value but captures obj_1 by reference

Let's see above example with lambda expression.

Example:

```
int main () {
        auto call_x = [] (int x) {
if (x > 5)
    cout<<x<<" is greater than 5"<<endl;
else
    cout<<x<<" is less than or equal to 5"<<endl;
};
        call_x (100);
return 0;
}
```

You can explore different flavors of writing lambda expression on google or ChatGPT.

In this I as an author explains you the need and its application by an example in this book.

29.3 Hausaufgaben

- Study advance feature of C++11. See more or explore more on www.google.com or use ChatGPT for specific concept.
- Explain the difference between C++ and C++11 specifications.

NOTES

Chapter 30
Threads in C++11

Introduction

In previous chapter we understand the why we need C++11 specification in C++ altogether. Here we see some more specifications added to C++ language. These are most important and considered are major addition to C++. And this addition is nothing but addition of threads concept to it. You wonder that then in previous versions how parallel or simultaneous work is achieve? Super computer design with old technique doesn't have this. In old generation computers do this with exploiting operating system feature and not by any language specific feature as far as C and C++ concerns. This introduction of threads is answer to usage task and pthread or POSIX library on Linux platform. So, these tools are not generic and needs rework. Or developer use some other language feature in conjunction with C++ to have parallelism or concurrency in application.

The introduction of threads is simple to implement and much generic in design. Since kernels of many operating systems are written in C and C++ language. The parallelism is achieved by writing micro or macro services in to application. With introduction of threads, it is achieved with single binary or executable.

30.1 Threads in C++11

Threads in C++ are used for concurrent or parallel programming. Even in latest architecture main method is also called using thread mechanism. When you execute application will run as a single threaded application with main method as a thread. Main method has its own thread id also called process id. Since it is parent thread of all threads created or forked from main process. Each thread has its own thread id and shared memory space of parent process. Each thread has its id, a set of registers, the stack pointer, the program counter, and the stack. However, threads share resources with one another within the process they belong to. In particular, they share the processor, memory, and file descriptors. If you have seen programming microcontroller you find that to switch to subroutine,we have to store address of last instruction and while end of routine we pop that address, threads do some similar work and executes independently. Below figure 30.1 shown C++11 thread lifecycle diagram.

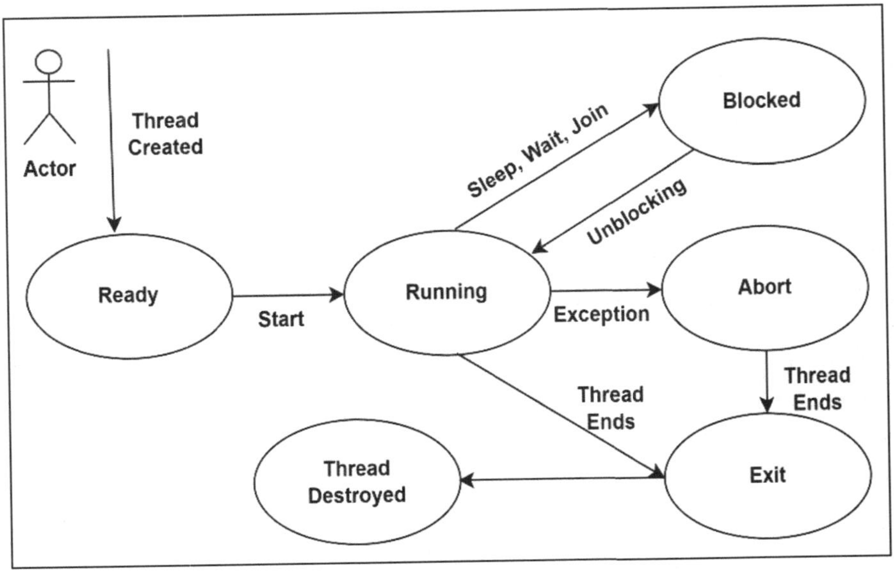

Figure 30.1 C++11 Thread Life Cycle

In C++11 threads are created by thread class. To use thread class developer, have to include "<thread>" header file. This header file provides all features to create thread and managing thread lifecycle.

First, when we create thread using thread constructor, then thread will come to ready state. Then thread from ready state to running state taken upon execution of application. Upon which thread will be moved to blocked state by calling sleep, wait and join call. Thread will be in running state upon unblocked state by calling wake call. Lifecycle of thread will be terminated upon its completion of execution or by calling exit in thread. Thread will be destroyed and no thread id available for reference to thread. Id will be cleared from memory. Thread will be aborted on exception thrown and it taken to exit cycle. Threads are lightweight to use and does developer ease of job for parallel programming. With multiprocessor architecture computation become really fast as processor have lesser job to do in computing result.

We use thread in two different scenarios, one will be for asynchronous call and other will synchronous (keep alive) call. What I mean by asynchronous call is thread is created say fired and it does its job and then exit immediately i.e. forget. I say in other manner that thread is fired and forget job i.e. single shot thread. It comes to exit state without repeating it execution. There won't be any blocked state. Its other counterpart is it remains alive until job from it is needed. Like say reading data on serial port of RS232 or RS485 or GPS data thread etc. I call them as a synchronous or keep alive thread.

Example of synchronous call is wait until we get reply from its service call. Control of execution could not move further to next instruction. It remains in blocked state at that instruction.

Example of asynchronous call is it won't wait until we get reply from its service call. Control of execution would move further to next instruction. Even thread remain or may not remain in blocked state. Its main thread keeps on execution its job.

How to create thread?

To create thread, first include "<thread>" header file and then create thread class instance and pass callable as an argument to thread constructor. Callable can be function, lambda expression or functor.

Syntax:

```
std::thread th (callable, arg1, arg2, ...)
th.join ();   //or
th.detach ();
```

Example:

```
void download_file () {
        // logic to download file from internet
    }

void monitor_progress () {
        //use timer to monitor time needed.
    }

int main () {
    std::thread fileDownloadThread (download_file);
        std::thread progressMonitorThread (monitor_progess);
        fileDownloadThread.join ();
```

```
                progressMonitorThread.join ();
            cout<<" Download Completed." <<endl;
    return 0;
        }
```

30.1.1 Thread APIs

join ():

Calling join over thread will block calling thread until the thread finishes.

detach ():

Calling detach over thread will not block calling thread and it continues execution without waiting for the thread to finish.

30.1.2 Thread Issues.

With advantage of concurrency of execution, thread faces synchronous or simultaneous access issue. There is lot more chances that it goes onto deadlock or give invalid intermittent result. To avoid these do not call same thread inside one another thread leads deadlock. Also to get valid intermittent result use mutex on that critical section or say on atomic variable inside thread callable.

One practical scenario I faced during my project work is thatI am using "zmq pair" socket. I am able to receive and send data. Further progress in work needs more threads to send and receive data. Suddenly one day this code of socket programming start throwing exception. At first, I really don't understand that my working code start crying and losing my hope. And afterday it starts happening every day. My seniors are not happy. After two days of debugging and verifying code, I come to conclusion that, we are pushing data and reading simultaneously from thread resulting into runtime exception required in synchronizing mechanism. And I tell you adding mutex lock to receive and send Apis solve problem I am facing and it never happened again. Adding mutex lock to critical section plays vital role for your application using threads.

Example:

Study this example of print i in thread with and without mutex. Also try vary sleep period and see output.

```
#include <iostream>
#include <thread>
#include <mutex>
```

```
using namespace std;
int i = 0;
mutex mtx;
void increment_i_one (int &arg) {
    while (arg < 100) {
        lock_guard<mutex> lock(mtx);
        arg++;
        this_thread::sleep_for(chrono::milliseconds(1));
    }
}
void increment_i_two (int &arg) {
    while (arg < 100) {
        lock_guard<mutex> lock(mtx);
        arg++;
        this_thread::sleep_for(chrono::milliseconds(1));
    }
}
void print_i (int &arg) {
    while (arg > -1 && arg < 100) {
        lock_guard<mutex> lock(mtx);
        cout<<"arg = "<<arg;
        this_thread::sleep_for(chrono::milliseconds(1));
    }
}
int main () {
    cout << "In threaded World!" << endl;
    thread th1 (increment_i_one,ref(i));
```

```
    thread th2 (increment_i_two,ref(i));
    thread th3 (print_i,ref(i));
    th1.join();
    cout<<"\nth1"<<endl;
    th2.join();
    cout<<"\nth2"<<endl;
    th3.join();
    cout<<"\nth3"<<endl;
    return 0;
}
```

Output:

```
In threaded World!
arg = 100
th1 th2 th3
```

30.2 default and deleted member function

- default keyword:

"default" keyword is used to declare special member functions as default member function. Such as default constructor is provided by compiler. One more function is a copy constructor, copy assignment operator and destructor are can be marked as default member function as they are provided explicitly by compiler rather implemented by developer. Once marked default, its implementation are provided by compiler.

Syntax:

```
Class DC {
public:
        DC () = default; //Default Constructor
        DC (DC&) = default; //Copy Constructor
        DC& operator = (DC&) = default; //Copy Assignment
};
```

Example:

```
#include <iostream>
using namespace std;
class DefaultMember {
public:
    DefaultMember () = default;
    DefaultMember (DefaultMember&) = default;
    DefaultMember& operator = (DefaultMember&) = default;
    DefaultMember (int i) {
        cout<<"Parameterized i = "<<i<<endl;
    };
    void show () {
        cout<<"Show Called."<<endl;
    }
};
int main () {
    DefaultMember dm;
    dm.show();
    DefaultMember dm_p (100);
    dm_p.show();
    return 0;
}
```

Output:

```
Show Called.
Parameterized i = 100
Show Called.
```

In example above we cannot mark show () = default; and compiler is not at all aware of its implementation.

- delete keyword

In contrary to default keyword, we have “delete” keyword. This is useful whenever developer not needed default implementation

for special member function as mentioned in case of default keyword. This is very much useful in case of singleton type class implementation. We don’t need to call copy constructor, copy assignment operator and use of move semantics.

Another advantage of marking function as delete that it doesn’t allow type promotion. Function with argument “int” is not promoted to “double” if type double is mentioned. Separate implementation is needed for double type. DefaultMember (int idm) is not get promoted to DefaultMember (double fdm). To understand this more consid er home automation system where you want to control brightness of LED bulb. Now brightness varies with integer number and input to controller goes double value, in this situation controller may truncate double and change brightness of LED bulb. This practice of varying brightness is not correct. End user should get restricted feeding wrong Delete keyword must be the 1st statement in class public section with delete keyword we can handle situation correctly.

Example:

```
class DeleteMember {
public:
        DeleteMember (float value) = delete;
        DeleteMember (int value) {
        // code goes below
        cout<<" Value =" <<value;
        }
};
int main () {
        DeleteMember idm (100);
        DeleteMember fdm (10.2f); //gives error since deleted
        Return 0;
}
```

Output:

```
Value = 100
```

30.3 override identifier

In the previous example we see that delete keyword is used to avoid integral type promotion and its consequences. As we know C++ is very strict about its type. Here override identifier is used in case of virtual functions. Now we know that if we give int data type in function signature and pass promoted type such as float data type then compiler gives warning and invoke that function or call such a function by truncating information pass. This scenario is observed in case of virtual functions. Now to tell compiler that we don't need integral promotion in function signature and signature should exactly match then we can achieve this by specifying override identifier in its derived implementation.

Consider real life example where we have online ticket booking platform on which we book for railways, airplanes or say road commute. Let's see in diagram,

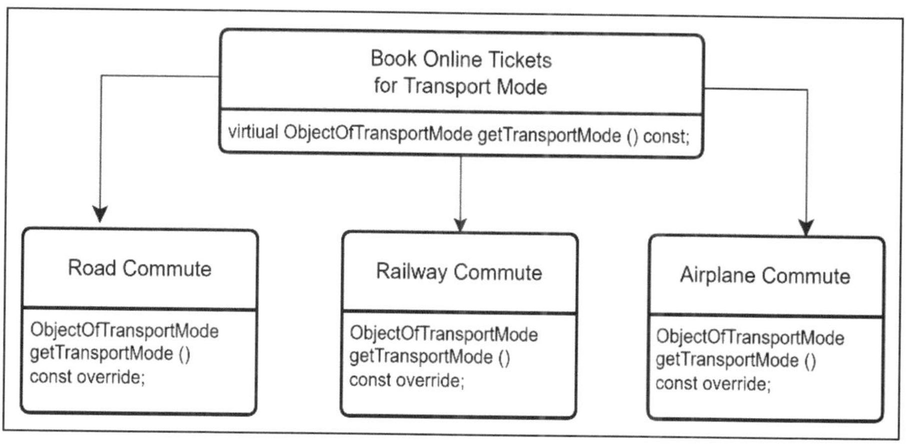

Figure 30.2 override identifier

Example:

```
class TransportMode {
public:
    virtual ~TransportMode () {}
    virtual TransportMode& getTransportMode () const = 0;
    virtual void showMode () = 0;
```

```
  void showTransportMode () {
    cout<<" Transport Mode Invoked Base"<<endl;
  }
};
class RailTransportMode : public TransportMode {
public:
  TransportMode& getTransportMode () const override {
    static RailTransportMode mode;
    return mode;
  }
  void showMode () override {
    cout<<" RailTransportMode "<<endl;
  }
  void showRailTransportMode () {
    cout<<" Rail Transport Mode Invoked Derived"<<endl;
  }
};
class AirPlaneTransportMode : public TransportMode {
public:
  TransportMode& getTransportMode () const override {
    static AirPlaneTransportMode mode;
    return mode;
  }
  void showMode () override {
    cout<<" AirPlaneTransportMode "<<endl;
  }
};
```

```
class RoadTransportMode : public TransportMode {
public:
   TransportMode& getTransportMode () const override {
      static RoadTransportMode mode;
      return mode;
   }
   void showMode () override {
      cout<<" RoadTransportMode "<<endl;
   }
};
int main () {
   TransportMode *mode = new RailTransportMode ();
   mode->getTransportMode().showMode();
   //calling derived since virtual
   mode->showTransportMode(); //calling base version
   // mode->showRailTransportMode (); error in line for above //line, not
   possible to call non-virtual method via base object
   delete mode;
   mode = new AirPlaneTransportMode ();
   mode->getTransportMode().showMode();
   delete mode;
   mode = new RoadTransportMode ();
   mode->showMode();
   delete mode;
   return 0;
}
```

Output:

```
RailTransportMode
```

Transport Mode Invoked Base

AirPlaneTransportMode

RoadTransportMode

30.4 Summary

- In this we come across most importantly as threads and then we saw use of delete, default keyword and override identifier.
- Explore unordered containers in google. These are built in library to store objects with fast retrieval access. We can use in case of less complexity.

Chapter 31

Advance Feature of C++ 14 Specifications

Introduction

After introduced standard for C++11, C++ committee shortly announce or introduce some more feature as a language specification to compete modern and feature development requirement in C++ language in year 2014. And they known as C++14 minor revision specifications for C++. C++14 introduced several new features and improvements over C++11.

31.1 Key features and changes in C++14

- Binary Literals
- Digit Separators
- Boolean and Integer Literals
- The gets () Function Was Removed
- Generic Lambdas
- Generalized Lambda Captures
- "auto" Return Type Deduction
- Aggregate Member Initialization
- Variable Templates
- Relaxed "constexpr" Restrictions
- The "std::make_unique"
- The "std::exchange" algorithm
- new and delete Elisions
- decltype (auto)
- Quoted Strings (std::quoted)
- Shared mutexes and locking

- tuple Addressing via type
- Heterogeneous Lookup in Associative Containers
- The Standard User-Defined literals
- "integral_constant" and "integral_constant ()" operator
- The is_final Type Trait
- The new begin – end iterators (rbegin – rend, crbegin – crend)
- The Integer Sequence (std::integer_sequence)
- The Member Initializers and Aggregates
- The New Overloads for Ranges
- Discourage rand ()

31.2 Binary Literals

Binary literals allow writing binary numbers directly using 0b or 0B prefix.

Example:

```
int binary_no = 0b1111
//....15 in decimal
```

31.3 Digit Separators

Digit separators improve readability of large numbers by allowing single quotes as digit separators.

Suppose developer or programmer wants to define delay in Mili or Micro-seconds can use this technique. This is very handy as we read digits.

Example:

```
int bigNum = 9'999'999
//.... 9999999
```

31.4 Generic Lambdas

Generic lambdas can be templated by using auto in the parameter list.

To develop calculator like Application or any string addition we perform generic lambda expression for this compiler generate code.

Example:

```
auto sum = [] (auto a, auto b) {return a + b;};
```

31.5 Automatic Return Type Deduction

By using "auto" keyword allows functions to deduce return type automatically.

Here in below, t_auto variable can be user-define type, constant or primitive data-type. Depend upon type auto keyword determine its variable data-type. This is very helpful in case of iterating over map or vector or list where long syntax or confusion of looking at syntax is redundant by using auto keyword, thus minimizing expression.

Example:

```
auto function_name () { return t_auto; }
```

31.6 Relaxed Constraints on "constexpr"

constexpr functions can now contain more complex statements like conditionals and loops.

Example:

```
constexpr int summation (int n_upto) {
   int result_sum = 1;
   for (int count = 0; count <= n_upto; ++count) {
      result_sum = result_sum + count;
   }
   return result_sum;
}
```

31.6.1 Declaring Member Functions with constexpr

Developer wants to return a constant from member function, such expression resulting constant is marked by keyword constexpr.

Example:

```
constexpr int class_name::getConstValue() const { return 100;
}
```

31.6.2 Variable Templates

Apart from C++11 templatized class, C++14 introduce creation of templated variables. By specifying type of template variable, it gets converted to type specific expression would be process later.

Example:

```
template<typename T>
constexpr T pi = T (3.14159265358979323 85);
double pi_x = pi<double>;
                    // 3.1415926535897932385
```

31.7 Attributes deprecated

Introduction of [[deprecated]] attribute is used to mark deprecated features. By marking function deprecated compiler generate warning message for such API. If any optimization

Example:

```
[[deprecated ("Use new_function() instead")]]
void deprecated_function();
```

31.8 make_unique

std::make_unique added to the standard library for creating std::unique_ptr instances.

Example:

```
auto uniue_ptr = std::make_unique<int>(10.99);
```

31.8.1 shared_timed_mutex

A new type of mutex that allows timed locking and shared ownership. shared_timed_mutex mutex;

Suppose it's a requirement of product to designed in such a way that connecting to remote server or cloud should not go more that specified requirement. Now to hold critical variable lock that cannot be last long than expected time frame. If we want to close network connection which last long due to network traffic say sending and validating OTP, we preferred to use time bound mutex on connection. As soon as we get connection within time frame it is advantageous to use shared_time_mutex. It gets destroyed on reaching specified time limit releasing resource acquired.

31.9 Chrono Literals

User-defined literals for duration and time points are defined by "<chrono.h>" header file for chrono library.

auto duration = 10s; // 10 seconds

Following are chrono literals define for time durations as below,

h = hours (nh where n = 1…n)

min = minutes (nmin where n = 1…n)

s = seconds (nsec where n = 1…n)

ms = mili-seconds (nms where n = 1…n)

us = micro-seconds (nus where n = 1…n)

ns = nano-seconds (ns where n = 1…n)

31.10 equal_to and Other Functors

Transparent comparators for standard library components like map, set. set<int, less<>> set = {1, 2, 3};

31.10.1 exchange

Utility function for exchanging the values of two objects.

int a = 500, b = 1000; exchange (a, b);

31.10.2 quoted

Manipulator for quoting and unquoting strings during I/O operations.

cout << quoted ("Welcome to C++ 14 Specifications!") << endl;

31.11 Lambda Capture Initializers

Allows lambdas to initialize their captures.

Example:

int x = 10;

auto lambda = [x = z + 1] () {return x;};

```
// x is initialized to z + 1
```

31.12 Aggregate Member Initialization

Allows aggregate classes to be initialized using brace-enclosed initializer lists.

Example:

```
struct Data {int x; double y;};
Data obj_d = {1, 2.3};
```

31.13 Tuple Addressing via get with Type

Allows accessing tuple elements by type. Tuple comes under std namespace. Use "using namespace std;"

Example:

```
tuple <int, double, string> person (100, 99.9, "C++14");
auto lang = get<string> (person);
```

31.14 std::make_reverse_iterator

Utility to create reverse iterators more conveniently.

Example:

```
vector<int> v_space = {100, 200, 300, 500};
auto rev_it = std::make_reverse_iterator(v_space.end());
```

31.15 Heterogeneous Lookup in std::map and std::set

Allows std::map and std::set to perform lookups with types different from their key type, if the comparison function supports.

Example:

```
it.std::map<std::string, int> complex =
                                   {{"real", 1}, {"img", 2}};
auto it = complex.find("real");
```

31.16 User-Defined Literals for std::string

Allows defining literals for std::string and std::string_view.

Example:

```
using namespace std::literals;
auto s = "Welcome to C++14"s;
```

31.17 Standardizing decltype(auto)

decltype (auto) was introduced to deduce the type of an expression, preserving the value category (i.e., lvalue or rvalue).

Example:

```
auto x = 10;
decltype(auto) y = (x); // y is an int&
```

31.18 is_final Type Trait

A new type to check if a class is marked as final.

Example:

```
struct structA final {};     or     class classA final {};
static_assert (std::is_final<classA>::value, "classA is not final");
```

31.19 Summary

In this chapter we have seen and explore specifications or features added to C++14 from C++. These are minor improvements and easy to use for developer to reduce development time features are added. As specially improvements for lambda, addition of chrono header file and auto keyword and others are primarily important improvements in C++14 releases.

NOTES

Chapter 32

Advance Feature of C++ 17 Specifications.

Introduction

Before moving deep into C++17 specification, we just look back and try to conceptualize what we know. So far, we see threads, containers and other added features as butter on cake. Now I want to talk about something about container in C++. All we know that C is functional programming language and data moves openly around system. Abstraction to data is comparatively less than that of techniques are used in C++ as a oops language. C++ is a object oriented language and data moves closely coupled to system. This is one important feature that language specifies. Other is encapsulation means data is inside packet (and not TCP packet). I mean to say in container. If we look C there is no such a feature. To pass data between functions and different classes we can use C style or C++ style. So many developers I saw uses C style to pass information between modules. I as an author of this and in my developer carrier I does the same until I understood container concepts and its use-case. I want to loudly told to all developers that use contains to exchange information between modules. The advantage of this technique is that you information is safely and in protected manner is communicated to different modules even you pass primitive types. Why I am saying that because I am comparing C with C++. The advantage is that your info is accessible only to those modules which contains container object and data inside it. It means that those modules which do not hold container can't access your data or information you pass to different modules in your programming design. It is very safe way to pass info with low risk and less damage to info. This is the encapsulated way of C++ as a OOPs principle. Information gets damage very less likely than C way of passing to different modules.

C++17 is one of the many iterations of the C++ programming language, designed to bring more robust features and improvements to developers.

Here are some of the key highlights of C++17 specifications.

32.1 Improved Standard Library

std::optional:

Used to represent optional values.

In this optional technique we use "std::nullopt" keyword to represent optional return type which is not considered from its list of occurrence. This technique is mostly useful in search algorithm where any value in record is considered as optional value. By looking at below example we have figure out optional entries in our student id record. Suppose in current academic record we have senior student ids from previous batch can be marked as optional and can be removed or updated by finding such a optional record.

Example:

```
#include <iostream>

#include <optional>

int main () {

std::optional<int> student_id[10] = {

1,2,3,4, std::nullopt,6,7,8,9,std::nullopt

};

int index_ = 0;

for (auto optional_id : student_id) {

index_++;

if(optional_id == std::nullopt) {

std::cout<<"Optional Student ID index is "<< index_<<"\n with optional value as "<< optional_id.has_value() <<std::endl;

}//if closed

}//for loop closed

return 0;

}//main closed
```

Output:

Optional Student ID index is 5

with optional value as 0

Optional Student ID index is 10

with optional value as 0

Example:

```
if(optional_id)
```

//change above example to this and re-run code and see o/p

Output:

Optional Student ID index is 1

with optional value as 1

Optional Student ID index is 2

with optional value as 1

.

.

.

Optional Student ID index is 8

with optional value as 1

Optional Student ID index is 9

with optional value as 1

In the above solution we have successfully filtered out optional record. With this we can insert those record into separate files.

std::variant:

A type-safe union to handle multiple types.

By looking at type it is easy to figure out that something represents or hold multiple or variant type information in single container of variant type.

Example:

```
#include <iostream>
#include <variant>
#include <string>
```

```
// Function to process different types of data
//this example is taken from online source.
Void process_data(const std::variant<int, float, std::string> & data) {
   std::visit([](auto&& arg) {
      using T = std::decay_t<decltype(arg)>;
      if constexpr (std::is_same_v<T, int>) {
         std::cout << "Integer: " << arg << std::endl;
      } else if constexpr (std::is_same_v<T, float>) {
         std::cout << "Float: " << arg << std::endl;
      } else if constexpr (std::is_same_v<T, std::string>) {
         std::cout << "String: " << arg << std::endl;
      }
   }, data);
}
int main () {
   std::variant<int, float, std::string> my_data;
   // Assign different types of data to the variant
   my_data = 42;
   process_data(my_data);
   my_data = 3.14f;
   process_data(my_data);
   my_data = std::string("Welcome to C++17!");
   process_data(my_data);
   return 0;
}
```

std::any:

Holds single values of any type.

With this std::any keyword, as name suggest developer represent any type of information like void pointers in C and C++. This is more object-oriented way to hold any type of information that is supported by language.

Example:

```
#include <iostream>
#include <any>
#include <string>
#include <typeinfo>
class Student {
public:
   void about_type() {
      std::cout<<"I am Student Type"<<std::endl;
   }
};
class Employee {
public:
   void about_type() {
      std::cout<<"I am Employee Type"<<std::endl;
   }
};
void print_about_any(const std::any& a) {
   if (a.type() == typeid(Student)) {
      std::any_cast<Student>(a).about_type();
   } else if (a.type() == typeid(Employee)) {
      std::any_cast<Employee>(a).about_type();
   } else if (a.type() == typeid(std::string)) {
std::cout << "I am String Type"  <<          std::any_cast<std::string>(a) <<
std::endl;
```

```
    } else {
        std::cout << "Unknown type" << std::endl;
    }
}
int main() {
    std::any a;
    // Store a Student in the any container
    a = Student();
    print_about_any(a);
    // Store a Employee in the any container
    a = Employee();
    print_about_any(a);
    // Store a string in the any container
    a = std::string("\nstd::any type is interesting");
    print_about_any(a);
    return 0;
}
```

Output:

```
I am Student Type
I am Employee Type
I am String Type
std::any type is interesting
```

Parallel Algorithms:

Introduces parallel algorithms to leverage multi-core processors. Refer google or ask your guide for how you can implement this. It is very simple but try on multicore processor.

32.2 Language Enhancements

Structured Bindings:

Allows the unpacking of tuples and other types. In C++17, a std::tuple is a fixed-size collection of heterogeneous values. Essentially, it's a way to group different types of values into a single object. This can be useful when you need to return multiple values from a function or when you want to handle a collection of mixed types more conveniently.

A std::tuple allows you to store a collection of values of varying types in a single object. Each element in the tuple can be of a different type, and the size of the tuple is fixed at compile-time.

Example:

```
#include <iostream>
#include <tuple>
#include <string>
std::tuple<int, std::string, double> get_employee_data() {
   return {1, "Girish", 59999.85};
}
int main() {
 // Using structured bindings to unpack the tuple
 auto [id, name, salary] = get_employee_data();
std::cout << "Employee ID: " << id << std::endl;
std::cout << "Employee Name: " << name << std::endl;
std::cout << "Employee Salary: " << salary << std::endl;
 return 0;
}
```

Inline Variables:

Facilitates defining and initializing variables directly in header files.

C++17 introduced the concept of inline variables, which allows the definition of a variable in a header file without violating the One Definition Rule (ODR). This can be particularly useful for constants that are defined in header files.

```
inline constexpr int MAX_CONNECTIONS = 100; inline constexpr double PI = 3.141592653589793;
```

If and Switch with Initializers:

Extends the syntax of if and switch statements to include initializers. It is very easy see guide help

Fold Expressions:

Simplifies template metaprogramming by reducing variadic template arguments.

Fold expressions in C++17 simplify and enhance the use of variadic templates by allowing you to apply binary operators to a parameter pack. This makes it easier to write more concise and readable code.

There are two types of fold expressions:

unary and binary.

Unary Fold Expression:

It involves summation (+) of different variadic types together.

We can use this in calculator for coding integer bill amount.

Example:

```
// Unary fold expression to sum all arguments

template<typename... Args>

auto summation
(Args... args) {

   return (... + args);

}
```

Binary Fold Expression:

Binary fold expression to multiply all arguments with an initial value

```
#include <iostream>

#include <initializer_list>

template<typename... Args>

auto multiply(int init, Args... args) {

   return (init * ... * args);

}
```

Refer previous example for binary fold expression

32.3 New Attributes and Features

[[nodiscard]]:

Warns when a function return value is ignored.

With this attribute we ensure that return value from any API is not ignored otherwise compiler generates warring message for that class or function. This is very helpful in good coding practises.

Example:

```
[[nodiscard]] int main () {
    //no return type specified cause warning message
// return 0;
}
```

Example:

```
#include <filesystem>
using namespace std::filesystem;
class [[nodiscard]] FileSystemCode {
public:
  FileSystemCode(int fcode) : fscode(fcode) {}
  int getFileSystemCode() const { return fscode; }
private:
  int fscode;
};
[[nodiscard]] FileSystemCode fileExists(const std::string &file) {
    std::filesystem::path file_path = file;
    if (std::filesystem::exists(file_path)) {
      return FileSystemCode (0);
    }
    return FileSystemCode(-1);
```

```
}
int main () {
 const std::string &filePath =
"/home/author/illLogicalThinkingInCandC++.pdf";
 //ignoring the return value to demonstrate the warning
    fileExists(filePath); //issue here to not handle return.
    return 0;
}
```

[[maybe_unused]]:

Suppresses warnings on unused entities.

How we can explain this is that there are OS specific calls in our application like flash OS on beagle board hardware. Now there is common information between the flashOS(filetoflash) method. Now there is argument to API which work on beagle board but not on AVR board. In such a case argument on AVR platform generate warning message by compiler. To suppress compiler warning developer, use this feature in application. But sometimes it is dis-advantage to suppress this warning rather to get notified with development issue.

Example:

```
void flashOS([[maybe_unused]] const char *filetoflash) {
            #ifdef __Apple__
                        //To Do filetoflash
#else
    // To Do
#endif
}
```

32.4 Usability Improvements

Filesystem Library:

Enhances filesystem manipulation capabilities with tools for paths, files, and directories. With filesystem we can monitors files in project folder. Suppose there are video files are logging continuously on drive and after a week duration drive becomes full and OS become unresponsive. These files are of no use after sometime comparatively. Solution to this problem is you free the space by uploading files on cloud or remove from drive so that OS become responsive and there is further logging possible smoothly. Such operations related to disk drive are possible with filesystem library.

Header file used for file system related operation is "<filesystem>"

Example:

```
#include <iostream>

#include <filesystem>

 namespace fs = std::filesystem;

 int main() {

  fs::path currentPath = fs::current_path();

  std::cout << "Files in " << currentPath << ":\n";

for (const auto& entry fs::directory_iterator(currentPath)) {

      std::cout << entry.path() << '\n';

  }

  return 0;

}
```

Splicing for Maps and Sets:

Efficiently moves elements between containers without creating temporary objects.

As a author, I can say confidently that once you master C++11, C++14 and C++17 specifications rest you can easily handle on your own. You don't find much difficulties in understanding C++20 and higher specifications. You have already master one level.

Here I stop my journey to C++. Thank you ☺

THE END

My Thought on Covid-19 situation

The book is written during covid-19 down lock period in July 2020 months, so feel proud about sharing thoughts written on covid-19 with name and for car shed

1. Save Trees, Dear Kavi Samelan on Elections

   Kavlyanchya kavitani

   kavlyana nahi padat pharak

   Eka kavlya borobar bakiche

   kavle jatat udat

   Ladtat te mavle ani

   nusate kavita karoon

   udatat te kavle.

   Kavlyano Kavita karnya

   barobar aarey carshed

   vachavoon dakhavata

   aali aasati tar abhimanane

   bolo aasato

   Kavlyanche mavle zhale mhanun

   Urleya kavlani mavlyana

   pan kele kavle kavita karoon

   #SaveArreay Save environment Save Nature Save anything natural

   #it is written during array trees are cutdown purposely for political powers

2. Kam Corona Kam Karona

   Karona ab kam karona, bas krona,

   thoda aaram karona, population kam karona,

pollution kam karona, baat karona, thoda hasa karona,
thoda bahar ghooma krona, khodkam kam karona,
income jyada karona, corruption kam karona,
zhagada kam karona, hindu-muslim fight kam karona,
living standard jyada karona, shiksha aachhi karona,
jyada trees lagaya krona, thode gadhonko kam kiya karona,
India ko richest karona, nature ko achha karona,
thodi pak pak kam karona, covid ko kam karona,
karona ko kam karona, carona ko kam karona,
jyada saving and bright future karona kam ko save kiya karona